DARE
TO
LIVE

A Guide to the Understanding
and Prevention of
Teenage Suicide and Depression

Michael Miller
with
Debra Whalley Kidney

Published by:
Beyond Words Publishing, Inc.
Pumpkin Ridge Road
Route 3, Box 492-B
Hillsboro, OR 97123
Phone: 1-503-647-5109
Toll Free: 1-800-284-9673

The information contained in this book is intended to teach
parents and educators about teenage depression and suicide.
Dare to Live is not meant to be a cure for depression, nor
will it prevent teen suicide. This information should not
replace competent professional treatment or medical care.
The contents of the book are intended to be used as an
adjunct to a rational and responsible program prescribed
by a professional or doctor. The author and publisher are
in no way liable for any use or misuse of the material.
The case studies in this book are real; however, the names,
circumstances and locations have been substantially
changed to protect the anonymity and confidentiality
of all cases.

Printed in the United States of America by Arcata Graphics,
Kingsport, Tennessee

ISBN: 0-941831-22-1
Library of Congress Catalog Card Number: 89-061266

Cover design by Jerry Soga

For information on the *Dare to Live* program for your
school or group, please contact the *Dare to Live* office in
Vancouver, Washington (206) 695-6927.

Publisher's Note

Beyond Words Publishing, Inc. produces books of uncompromising standards and integrity, books that invite us to step beyond the limits of our experience to discover what lies within, beyond words.

Our publications include: children's, photographic, nature, self-help, health and psychology books, as well as calendars and audio tapes.

For a free catalog of our newest titles please contact:

Beyond Words Publishing, Inc.
Pumpkin Ridge Road
Route 3, Box 492-B
Hillsboro, OR 97123
503-647-5109
1-800-284-9673

A celebration of life through publishing.

Acknowledgments

The authors of this book want to gratefully acknowledge Dennis Elleson for his help with the drug and alcohol abuse chapter, Charlotte Kegley, Wendy Wood M.A. and Annette Selmer M.S. for their assistance with the sexual abuse information. Special thanks to Edith and Wayne Horne, Jodie Suckling, Beyond Words Publishing, our spouses, Katrina Miller and Dan Kidney, and our families who helped and encouraged us.

Table of Contents

*Dedicated to the family of Paul Horne
and to all teenagers and their parents.*

1

Introduction

"I have job security — and I wish I didn't."
— Michael Miller

Gresham Union High School
Gresham, Oregon
April 1988

The big auditorium is empty except for a few adults toward the front. One, a man in his middle thirties, paces in front of the stage, fiddles with a slide projector, and checks the clock. The students will be dismissed from class shortly for this special assembly. Now Michael Miller concentrates on the job ahead of him: speaking to 1,600 teenagers for an hour and a half about depression, suicide, and life.

A few students begin trickling in. The student body president comes forward, and she and Michael stand and visit as the bell rings and the kids pour through the doors. The noise level rises as the seats are filled and other students sit against the walls. Stepping forward to the mike, the student body president leads the school in the Pledge of Allegiance.

1

Her introduction is brief. "Today our assembly is presented by Michael Miller."

Michael vaults onto the stage and begins his outreach to the fidgety students. Within minutes they have settled into the presentation and are receptive to Dare to Live's message.

"First I want to give you the rules to this assembly. There are three rules. Number one is no talking. You personally may not need to hear what I have to say, but that doesn't mean that the friends around you don't need to listen to what I have to say, and if you're talking they are going to listen to you instead of me. So give them a chance to listen. O.K.?

"Rule number two really isn't a rule, it's permission. This thing is an hour and a half long; it is rather boring if I do say so myself. If you feel the need to go to sleep, go ahead. But try not to snore. Some of the guys, especially the big football types, can really, you know, be disruptive.

"And the third thing is, and I hesitate to say this, but I was at another high school a couple of weeks ago and a young lady in the front row fell asleep. She laid her head on her boyfriend's shoulder, and she drooled all over him. That's really disgusting. So, ladies, if you're going to go to sleep, stuff a tissue or something in your mouth if you have that problem.

"We're going to start with a slide presentation. This is a baby picture. How many of you knew that? Good; you've all studied health. Now, I'm the father of four children, and after having four children I've come to the conclusion that babies are only capable of doing five things. They are basically lumps, and all they can do is eat, sleep, cry, mess, and stink. But we all started out that way.

"This is a baby picture of a young man named Paul Horne. Paul was born in Tacoma, Washington, about 18 years ago, and this picture was taken of him when he was only a couple of hours old. . . ."

That's the way I begin my program called *Dare to Live*, and over the next hour and a half I tell kids about suicide, depression, living, and loving. I touch on the subjects of drug and alcohol abuse, sexual abuse, self-esteem, the warning signs of depression, and where they can go to find help. It is a mini-course on life, and since its beginning in 1985, my program has saved dozens of teens' lives.

Teen suicide is a raging epidemic in this country. It kills thousands of our children every year. Statistics help bring this reality into focus. Since 1960, the suicide rate in the 15- to 24-year-old age group has more than doubled, from 7.1 per 100,000 in 1960 to 15.6 per 100,000 in 1985. That means that more than 5,000 young people in this group kill themselves each year. The United States has the sixteenth highest suicide rate of all nations, and suicide is the second leading cause of death for 15- to 24-year-olds. The leading cause of death in this age group is accidents, but many suicides are counted as accidents because the survivors want it that way.

One 14-year-old drove his motorcycle into a tree at 85 miles per hour. Two days before he died he was called in by his math teacher because his grades were so bad that he was in danger of flunking. He told the teacher, "I don't care if I flunk or not, because I'm not going to live past the end of the year anyway." His death was listed as an accident.

Every suicide leaves six to 10 other victims — family and friends who must go on living. They feel abandoned, angry, and guilty. It takes these victims years to recover. Some never do.

Many suicides are covered up, and many suicide attempts are never revealed. Paul Horne, a young man whose story is central to my program, wrote in an essay that he had attempted to take his life once before. His mother, who read the essay after Paul's death, had no idea how or when. The second time he tried, he succeeded.

Estimates on the number of attempted suicides by teenagers range as high as 500,000 a year. Most experts say that there are 100 attempts for every success. I've been out there, in the hospitals and at the sites, and at first I was skeptical of this number. But in Clark County, Washington, where I live, a teen attempts suicide every other day. That means 183 Clark County students attempt suicide each year. Multiply that by 39 counties in Washington and the total for this medium-sized state is more than 7,100 attempts a year. There are 3,049 counties in the United States, and while my calculations may not be scientific, using Clark County as an "average" county brings the total number of teenage suicide attempts in the United States to 557,967 a year. That's overwhelming.

It is disturbing for parents to think they wouldn't know if their kids were in trouble, but many times they *don't* know. I was talking about the prevalence of teen suicide to a friend who has a teenager of his own. He was disbelieving, so he called his daughter in and asked her, "Emily, have you ever thought about taking your life?"

She looked at him as if he were crazy and said, "Yeah, I've thought about it. A month ago I was really depressed and I tried to kill myself." Kids are attempting suicide all the time. Parents rarely find out about the ones who try and fail. They know about the ones who succeed, or nearly succeed, because these teens have to be hospitalized or buried.

Throughout this book are excerpts from a typical assembly that I presented at Gresham Union High School in April 1988. The assembly is the vehicle that I use to reach the kids. It brings them the message of *Dare to Live* — a message that has saved the lives of many teenagers who were depressed, hopeless, and helpless to know what was wrong or how to fix it.

There are several reasons why *Dare to Live* has succeeded. First is that its purpose has always been to reach young people. My program has been turned down by many schools because they have already educated their teachers about teen suicide. The problem is that they forget to educate the students.

Second, *Dare to Live* succeeds because it reaches adolescents on their level. I communicate to them as 13-year-olds,

16-year-olds, or 18-year-olds. I tell stories that teens find funny, and I use examples they can relate to. I not only talk to them, but they receive my message.

Third, as you will see in this book, I am not approaching teen suicide from an academic or professional background. I am coming from a common-sense, practical-experience, I'm-a-parent-too background. I'm using the lessons I have learned in dealing with kids over the last 15 years.

What we discuss in this book is not deep, dark, mysterious, psychological mumbo-jumbo, or technical medical knowledge. The information is presented in a down-to-earth, easy-to-understand format so that parents, counselors, teachers, pastors, priests, administrators — *anyone* who works with or deals with teens — and especially the kids themselves can pick this up. It is meant to be a one-on-one study of suicide and depression, communication and love, respect and consideration for others.

The young people who are attempting and committing suicide are all around you. They are not just the ones who are disturbed because of terrible circumstances in their lives, although depression is much more likely among teens suffering through abusive situations. The main purpose of this book is to alert parents and teachers that the teen who kills himself or herself may be just like the one at your home or in your class. Meet three of these "typical" students. (Except in the case of Paul Horne and his family, all names of young people and their parents have been changed to protect their privacy.)

Molly

Molly has naturally curly brown hair, an open, friendly smile, and a willing-to-please attitude. I met with Molly and her parents, Janet and Mark, after she attempted suicide. Molly is the kind of young person who keeps most of her anxieties deep inside of her. She has a cheerful "everything's fine" demeanor that often covers how she is really feeling.

Most of Molly's pain began at school. "I'd walk by groups of people," she explains, "and they'd be talking about me. They'd say I had an afro, and because I'm tall, girls would spread rumors about me. They were just total snobs." Molly felt as if she didn't have any friends.

Her schoolwork began slipping, and Molly's teachers told her that they were going to call her parents. At home Molly heard her parents fighting with her older brother and sister; the tension from the anger between her parents and siblings also affected her. "I was worried and all nervous, and a whole bunch of things were piling up."

Molly says she tried to tell her friends how she felt, but when she did they would tell other kids and everyone would get mad. She didn't consider talking to her parents, brother or sister about her feelings. "I thought they'd say, 'It's all right; just ignore it,' but I couldn't do that. And my mom has a short temper. Whenever something goes wrong she yells at us. I wasn't sure I could talk to my dad. I wasn't used to talking to him at all; I was more used to talking to my mom."

After considering the situation, Molly decided to kill herself. "Then I wouldn't be around anybody, and I wouldn't have to think about those kinds of things, and I wouldn't be so nervous and scared." So one night she went into the bathroom and took between 30 and 40 Extra Strength Tylenol.

"I didn't want my parents to walk in and see blood all over my room or something," Molly says. "[And afterward] I went to my mom and told her I took a whole bunch of Tylenol and had a stomach ache. I threw up about three times and my mom called the poison center. They told her to take me to an emergency room."

Molly's mom, Janet, put the events together a little differently. When Molly began vomiting, she assumed her daughter had the flu. It wasn't until the next morning that she remembered Molly telling her that she had taken "lots" of Tylenol, and it was not until she was on the phone to the poison control center that she asked Molly exactly how many pills she had taken.

Molly was lucky. She had to spend several days in the hospital, but she did not have any permanent damage. She and her parents began seeing a counselor, and Molly is working on telling her family how she feels. Molly now says her attempt was "really kind of stupid," and she has learned some mechanisms to help her cope with the kids at school. "I know that people who talk about me aren't my friends. I know to stay away from them and be myself instead of trying to impress everyone."

Molly has done a lot of growing up in the five months since her attempt, but she also has a lot of growing up left to do, because she is still a little girl. Molly was 10 and a half years old and in the fifth grade when she overdosed.

Rob

The second time that I met Rob, a year after our first meeting, the circumstances were considerably different. I first spoke at Rob's high school during the spring of his junior year. He approached me after the program because a week earlier he had survived a suicide attempt but was still feeling desperate.

Rob is tall, well-built, and handsome. Now finishing his senior year, he is graduating with a 3.94 cumulative grade-point average (out of a possible 4.0) and is the class valedictorian. He has won honors in football and basketball and an appointment to the Naval Academy, where he hopes to pursue a career as a pilot. Talking to Rob on this day 11 months after he tried to kill himself, it seems impossible to believe that anything could have driven this confident, well-adjusted, successful student so close to death. I will let him tell his story.

Rob's problems began with his girlfriend. "I'd been going out with Erin for a little less than a year, and it wasn't working out. We were arguing, she'd get mad at me for everything, and I had it in my mind that we should break up. Then I found out she was pregnant."

The news did nothing for the shaky relationship. Rob shouldered his responsibility, he and Erin discussed the alternatives, and they agreed that an abortion was the logical solution. The young couple scrambled to come up with the money, and during this time Rob says they fought even more.

After the pregnancy was terminated Rob broke up with Erin. "I broke up with her, but I still talked to her and associated with her because I wanted to make sure she was o.k. But I guess I didn't do a good enough job of it. I just didn't know what I was supposed to do, because I'd never been through it before."

Erin was bitter following the abortion and breakup. She began talking about Rob to her friends, and rumors about him began circulating through the school. "The rumors that were started about me were really bad. My friends would come up to me and ask, 'So, Rob, I heard this about you. Is it true?' I traced the rumors back to Erin and her friends."

Soon another of Rob's friends became involved in the situation. Kelly was a good friend of both Rob and Erin, but Erin began to hate Kelly because she still associated with Rob. "Erin thought I didn't deserve any friends," Rob says. When Kelly's difficulties with Erin continued, Rob felt responsible for dragging an innocent party into the mess.

"I was feeling pretty down because Kelly was going through some bad times that I believed were my fault. I thought if I weren't around, Erin wouldn't have anybody to pick on and start rumors about because the cause of the problem would be gone. And Erin wouldn't hate Kelly, and Kelly would get back together with all her friends."

To Rob the easiest solution was to kill himself. Rob never tried to talk to anyone about his painful feelings before his attempt. He thought about suicide for a few weeks, and then one weekend, with his parents out of town and his sister away at college, the opportunity was there.

"I was in the bathroom brushing my teeth and the medicine cabinet was open. I saw all the pills in there, and I just took a few of each and a lot of aspirin, and I think some codeine. I just randomly dumped them in my hand." After taking the pills he went to his room, lay down, and became sick a little while later. Eventually he fell asleep, and then he woke up with a headache. "I really dragged for the rest of that day and the next, and I didn't feel too hot."

Rob says he felt some relief when he woke up and found he hadn't died, because he realized that he couldn't do that to his parents. "What would they do if they came home and I was dead in my room?" he asks. "I couldn't believe I could do something that bad to my parents. But at the time I was only thinking about all the people at school."

A week later, following the *Dare to Live* assembly, Rob talked to me, I talked to the school counselor, and the counselor called Rob's mom. It was difficult for Rob to have to tell his mother about his problems. She contacted a psychiatrist to help Rob. It wasn't until four months later that the rest of Rob's family, his father and sister, found out about his attempt.

Rob explains his reluctance to tell his father about the suicide attempt. "I didn't want my dad to know about it. My dad's old-fashioned. He grew up on a farm and I guess he still thinks he's on one. The way he handles things is a little different: he yells. I don't like it and I don't like to make him mad. He just gets really unreasonable. I wrecked the car once and he took away my keys for six months.

"I knew he wasn't going to be forgiving. I thought he was just going to kill me. And he did yell. His reaction was basically what I expected. At first he yelled and screamed, 'How could you do that? How could you do something like that? I raised you up not to do things like that,' because he also heard about the mess with Erin.

"I told him, 'Well, I made a choice, dad, and I just made a mistake. It's my fault and it's my life.' He calmed down in about half an hour. I realize now that yelling is his way of caring. It's nice to know he's there and he cares. Before, I thought he was just there to yell; he was just a disciplinarian and didn't care how I did, he just yelled. But now I know he cares.

"My dad gave me a lecture on morals. I've been raised a Lutheran and premarital sex is against my religion. He was a little upset about that. I said, 'Dad, God forgives, can't you?' And he said, 'Yes, I can. It just takes me longer.'

"The psychiatrist told me I have to realize that I just screwed up. I made a mistake. It's a mistake I've got to live with for the rest of my life, but I don't have to think about it, and I know that I certainly don't have to die over it. I realize that now. There is help."

Stacie

Jean and Tom Turner, and their second daughter, Colleen, are sitting around the kitchen table. Jean and Colleen are smoking as they talk about Stacie, the youngest child in this close-knit family. Jean speaks carefully and deliberately about the tragic event that shook the family less than 10 months earlier. Colleen, who is 30, adds details or confirming evidence. Her emotions — anger, frustration, and grief — are revealed more often than her mother's as she talks about her little sister. Tom listens most of the time, and then quietly adds his ideas. When he speaks, his statements are thoughtful and concise.

It is obvious that this family has gone over this ground before. They have examined every nuance of every statement, considered every action. The details are familiar to all. One begins a story and another finishes it. Questions are probed from every angle, and yet the answers still elude. Maybe the answers will always be just out of reach. For a family that has lived through a teen suicide there are many, many questions and far fewer answers.

The Turners' story began in 1971 with the birth of their fifth child, Stacie Anne Turner. Stacie was born far from the family's home state during a period when Tom Turner's job had forced the family to relocate. The Turner children were separated into two distinct groups: the first three, two girls and a boy, had been born close together in age; then after a seven-year lapse, the two youngest girls, Amanda and Stacie, were born.

Being the youngest of this brood had its natural advantages. With three older siblings the perfect age and size for hauling around the littler ones, Stacie was doted upon. But in addition she was born with a fragile, benign facial tumor. It was removed later, but as a toddler she could not fall down for fear she would bump her face and cause it to bleed. Three youngsters and two adults danced attendance on the bright and busy one- and two-year-old Stacie.

Stacie grew comfortably within the warmth of her family cocoon. But even the most stubborn of butterflies are eventually forced to fly. For Stacie the first big change in her life occured when she was four. The Turners moved back to their home state, the older children began graduating from school and leaving home, and mother Jean went to work outside the home. In retrospect, Jean says this was a hard time for all the family, but maybe especially hard for Stacie.

The next year kindergarten beckoned, but there was a dilemma. Stacie's birthday fell on the cutoff date for school entry. She could enter, but she would be the very youngest in her class. Jean considers this decision 10 years later and shakes her head. "I think it was a mistake," she says. "She sailed through, she did wonderfully, but the school always said that while Stacie was right on intellectually, socially she was a year behind."

Her father has no doubts that his youngest child was the brightest of the family's children, but beginning as early as the fifth grade, she began having social problems. The problems Stacie Turner experienced were the same ones that hundreds of other young people experience every day: the push and pull of friendships, the struggle to balance expectations of relationships with the reality of being young and fickle, and the intense desire to be accepted by those one likes.

Her father says, "Stacie wanted friends, and yet she was really critical of those friends and their imperfections. When they did something wrong she would chastise them. In a way, she caused her own problems, but everybody does that. She was also kind of lazy. She wouldn't go out of her way to work on friendships, therefore the few she had were more important to her. And when something happened between them, it was very catastrophic."

Indeed, something catastrophic happened between Stacie and a close friend, Terri, the year both girls were juniors at a private high school. Terri attempted suicide. Stacie stayed right by her friend during this difficult time. She talked to Terri's mother regularly about how Terri was feeling and spent hours with Terri, putting herself on the line for a friend who was hurting. And that too fit into Stacie's profile.

"Stacie was a real helper," Jean says. "She was totally consumed with helping, not just Terri, but everyone. She was a giver."

Tom adds, "The only group Stacie had trouble with was her peer group. People older than her and younger than her, she just loved them and they loved her back."

Terri's cry for help seemed to "super-bond" Stacie to her. But three or four months after Terri's suicide attempt she began pushing Stacie away. Tom Turner: "One of the things that was so traumatic for Stacie was kids her own age rejecting her. It caused her a lot of pain," says her father

Colleen adds: "Stacie felt so bonded toward Terri. Here she thought she saved Terri's life. To Stacie, what better friend could you be? Then Terri wrote the letter."

The letter was Terri's attempt to break off her relationship with Stacie. Stacie took it hard. Her family lists other factors they now believe to have contributed to Stacie's depression. Her father had been laid off and without a job for over a year, her mother had recently had two operations, money was tight, the private school was demanding, and finals were just around the corner. Then an escapade with Terri and another friend ended with Stacie's hand badly hurt, but neither friend willing to stay and help her. To Stacie it must have seemed that her friends abandoned her during a time of need. Terri's subsequent letter rejecting Stacie's friendship was the last straw.

Jean explains, "I think Stacie was hurting real bad. Her sisters talked to her a lot, but even so, there was a new tone to Stacie's voice that made the hair stand up on the back of my neck. Two or three times I felt that, but I thought it's because she's a teenager, this is our fifth child who's gone through this. I was lulled into thinking that."

Colleen echoes this thought, "One time I even asked her, 'Stacie, are you thinking of suicide?' She looked at me and said, 'No,' and I turned around and walked off. I kept saying to myself, oh, she's just being 16."

Memorial Day weekend: Finals were looming at school, Stacie had recently been hired at a fast-food restaurant and was working 20 hours a week, and had been spending hours writing poetry and walking the floors late at night. Most of the family had left town for the holiday. Colleen and her family had gone to the mountains. Her father had left to target shoot. Her mom and an uncle were at home with Stacie and her sister Amanda.

"Stacie was asked to take Mandy to work so she could have the car," Jean says, "and she didn't want to take her. Stacie said, 'Don't let me have the car. Don't make me take her.' But Amanda had to be at work. Stacie seemed kind of depressed, I guess. She was harried. I thought it was school. She got ready to take Mandy. She took a bath and put on her school basketball sweatshirt. It's all really symbolic now. I helped her get ready. I brought her a towel and found her a clean bra. All these things;

now I think, oh my God, I helped her get ready. She got in the car with her sister. Obviously she had the gun that was under our mattress.

"At the front door she turned around and gave me the saddest little look. I guess the sadness that I will die with is that I didn't give her a hug. And that was it."

From what the family can piece together, Stacie left Amanda off at work and went to Terri's house. Terri was not there, but Stacie left a poem with her mom. She then went to see another friend, and the family believes there were angry words exchanged. Stacie left the second house and drove up to the top of a local viewpoint. It was the same place where Terri had attempted suicide. Stacie pulled her car over to the side of the road behind a taxi.

The taxi driver watched Stacie in his rearview mirror. He saw her bend over. He saw cigarette smoke, and then he heard what sounded like a rock dropping. Two men walking up the hill behind the car saw what had happened, and the taxi driver called the police. On Memorial Day, at 16 and a half, Stacie Turner shot herself and died.

On her lap was the letter from Terri. Copies of the following poem were left at Terri's house and sitting beside the phone at the Turner home:

You want to die when you're with me,
But I can't live without you, can't you see.
So, there is only one thing left for me to do
I have to do it to protect you.
Please understand, it's not your fault
I've felt this for awhile, and it's got to halt
But before I do, I'll give it one more try
But if it doesn't work then I'll say good-bye.
I am sorry to do it up there
But it's the only place I could figure where.

Because, you see I've had dreams too
But in them, this person doing this is me not you.
There is really nothing left here for me
And this is the way it has to be.
Please realize it's for the best
It really wasn't this problem it was all the rest.
The pressure just builds up and there's nothing to do.
Can't you see it's better to be me than you.
God I'll miss you.
Good-bye.

Colleen lights another cigarette and takes a deep breath. "At first when she died I'd think that if I could have her back I'd just hug her and tell her how much I loved her. Later I felt that I'd first tell her how much I loved her, and then I'd slap her. And now if she came back, I can't honestly say I wouldn't slap her first.

"I wish those who want to commit suicide could experience being dead for a week. I know her death affected her friends, but she wasn't thinking about us, about how much her family loved her. She was so tunnel-visioned with what she thought was important in her life. If she could just see . . . ."

Dare to Live

When I was 16 years old I decided to become a minister, and that desire marks the beginning of what is now the *Dare to Live* program. My calling has always been to help youth. I began working with a junior high Sunday School class when I was 19, and I have never looked back. Working with teens is still what I do best.

After high school I did the "normal" things. I joined the Navy and left the Navy. I went to Bible college and then left that to get married and have a family. (My wife Katrina and I have three daughters and a son: Heidi, Matthew, Hannah, and Katie.) I became a youth minister, and I knew that was really what I wanted to do. Then I got sidetracked and pastored for four years. (The advantage to working with kids is that if they don't like you, they'll tell you to your face. If an adult doesn't like you, he'll often smile and then tell everybody else what he really thinks about you.)

When you pastor a church, you can get stilted in your views. You work with Christians and talk mainly to Christians, so you have an unbalanced perspective on the real world. In the Bible, Jesus went out and talked to the multitudes. I felt I needed a way to get back into the community, to keep my ministry fresh. That is why I became a volunteer chaplain for Clark County Fire District Five.

As the chaplain it was my duty to go to the scene of major accidents, fires, and deaths to offer emotional support to the victims and survivors. To facilitate my work as chaplain I also became a volunteer fireman and volunteer Emergency Medical Technician.

It doesn't take long when you're working in emergency situations to see suicide and the results of attempted suicide. What struck me immediately was the number of young people who were taking their lives.

It haunted me to see kid after kid after kid attempt to take his or her life and to go to scenes where kids had successfully committed suicide. I remember the suicide of one 14-year-old girl. The day before she died her mother had taken her to the mall. It was a few days before school started, and they must have spent $1,000 on clothes. This teen had four pairs of $50 jeans, with the tags still on, laying on her bed, plus dresses and blouses, a whole wardrobe. That night she went outside, put her dad's pistol in her mouth and blew her head off. Her father found her the next morning when he went out to go to work, his gun still in her hand. When you see things like that it is obvious that suicide is a total waste. I felt a real need to reach these kids.

I talked to teens who were not as successful as the 14-year-old as they lay in hospitals recovering from attempts, and I detected a pattern to their actions. They were hurting, they had nowhere to go, and above all, they didn't understand their depression.

"Why didn't you talk to somebody about this?" I'd ask.

They would answer, "I didn't have anyone to talk to."

"Why didn't you call the fire department? I'm the chaplain. I would have talked to you."

"I didn't know that."

Or, "Why did you try to kill yourself?"

"Because I was flunking out of school."

The truth is that these teens were flunking out of school because they were depressed, and they were attempting suicide because of this same depression. They weren't depressed because they were flunking. They were looking at the symptoms rather than the cause. They weren't dealing with the cause of their depression because they didn't understand it.

It became a calling. I wanted to reach these kids and give them a chance to understand what was happening. Simply put, *Dare to Live* came from seeing a need that wasn't being met. I decided at that point that I no longer wanted to be a pastor.

Working with kids was what I liked to do and what I was good at doing, yet I didn't want to go back to youth pastoring and working with a small group. The idea for the *Dare to Live* program came to me one day while I was taking a shower. That's when I decided that I wanted to go into the schools and talk to students about teen suicide.

With my experience, I felt I could *do* something about this. I cared about kids, I related well with kids, I had talked to many kids who had problems, and I knew I could communicate basic common sense that would get through to them. I resigned my job as pastor and began finding out all I could about teen suicide.

I read everything I could lay my hands on. It was February1985, and there hadn't been much written on the subject. Few books had been published, but a lot of magazine articles covered what was beginning to be recognized as a national problem. I also checked out all the related psychology information that I could find.

Building on my library research, I went back and interviewed teenagers I had worked with over the last six years who had attempted suicide. I asked them what they wished they had known before their attempts, what they thought their friends should have known, and what could have been done to prevent their pain. I talked to parents, to counselors, and to ministers. I examined the issue from every conceivable angle.

I knew that if I wanted to go into the schools, I had to go in with absolutely the best program the schools had ever seen. First, I had to figure out exactly how to approach the subject. I knew I had to be able to sit down and talk to 25 teens, or 1,000-plus teens, at any given time about depression and suicide, without making the talk depressing in itself, *and* give them useful information. My talk even needed to be humorous. But how do you treat a subject like death lightly?

It took a lot of trial and error to figure out my approach. I would talk to kids and clarify their reasoning, and then bounce stories and ideas off my friend (and now associate) Jodie Suckling, her husband Tad, and my wife Katrina.

For the next step, I decided I needed a video presentation to use with the program. Jodie volunteered to write a script based on true stories from three teens who had attempted suicide. Then she found actors from the high school and community, located a video crew, and directed the production of the videotape.

After eight months I was confident I had a good and meaningful program. *Dare to Live* was not quite in the polished two-hour (or 90-minute) format that I use today. It was two days long! The seniors at Fort Vancouver High School in Vancouver, Washington, were my first "live" audience, and they sat through two hours on two consecutive days. I know the program reached them. I also realized that it had to be shortened.

When I approach schools about *Dare to Live*, or they contact me, they often react with stunned silence when I say that the assembly is an hour and a half long. It *is* difficult to schedule that much time outside the classroom, and I'm sympathetic to that problem. But if the school can't give me at least 90 minutes, I won't do the program. I feel that if I can't do a good and thorough job, I would rather not do it at all. I always wonder what they want me to leave out. Should I cut the part on the warning signs, or the part about where to go for help? Everything I say, even the funny stories, has a purpose; it is all vital to the *Dare to Live* message.

The program is not static; it is in a constant state of change. For example, depending on the audience I make changes in the program itself. I can tailor it to a junior high audience — I usually hit the sexual abuse problem harder — or an inner-city or suburban high school. I can also adjust the program to emphasize certain areas that a school may want to target, such as, drug and alcohol abuse, teen pregnancy, or self-esteem.

I have had to defend my program from the very beginning because everyone is a critic. I have heard that the program is too polished, it's not polished enough, it's too funny, it's too depressing. I can only reply that *Dare to Live* works, it reaches teenagers, and it saves lives.

Once the program was ready for presentation I was ready to go. But not all the schools were ready for me. Getting into schools is a struggle. First, the school must be realistic enough to admit they have a student suicide problem. Some administrators feel it is a weakness to say that they need help in this area. Second, competition is sometimes a problem. When one school or district has presented *Dare to Live* first, a neighboring school may not want to follow.

Many districts also think that if they merely teach their

staff about teen suicide, then the problems will be resolved. I contacted several school districts in a state where I planned on vacationing, because I thought it would be a good opportunity to introduce my program. They wrote back and said, "We had a workshop for our counselors and a psychologist came in. He told them all about teen suicide." *The problem is, no one bothered to tell the kids.* So the students were sitting over here hurting, and the counselors were over there saying, "We know about this problem." The program I've developed doesn't educate the counselors and teachers, because I assume they are already educated. I go directly to the kids.

I do talk to the teachers and counselors before I do a program in order to alleviate fears that the school will fall apart because I have talked about death, dying, and suicide. The teachers worry that students may come back from the auditorium a great big mess. They worry the program will be a huge bummer. So I tell them it is an uplifting, alive program and then answer questions.

Even after I have given an assembly I can get surprising responses from the adults. The principal at one high school looked at all the kids who wanted to talk to me and said, "Boy, you caused a lot of problems."

"No," I said, "the problems were already here. This just brought them to the surface." He wanted to be the ostrich with his head in the sand; he didn't see any problems because he wasn't looking for them. But you can't wait until a student commits suicide before you realize someone may be hurting.

When I first put this program together a great number of schools told me, "Yes, teen suicide is a national problem. But we don't have that problem here." That's ridiculous. How many schools would say, "We don't have a drug problem." Realistically, if you have a high school you have a drug problem. You also have sexual abuse problems, you have depression, and you have a suicide problem — *because kids hurt.* It matters not what neighborhood or economic strata they come from, or whether their religious affiliation is Christian, Jewish, Buddhist, or pagan; kids are kids are kids, and they hurt.

A lot of politics is involved in such a volatile issue. If there has been a suicide, people want to know why the program wasn't held earlier. Once, following a suicide, I was invited to a school by a counselor. But the program got nixed by the principal because he felt the student who died wasn't popular enough to warrant the assembly. If there hasn't been a suicide I face the classic denial, "We don't have a problem," or the superstition that talking about suicide will trigger it.

The myth that talking about teen suicide encourages it is just that, a myth. To talk about teen suicide in an educational, informative setting, in a factual, non-emotional, non-glorifying manner is good and healthy. The same can be said about sex education. If you talk about sex, do kids have sex in the halls? Not if you teach sex education in an informative setting and give the kids appropriate knowledge. The same is true about depression and suicide; the outcome of education depends on how you approach the subject.

Teen suicide should never be glorified or exalted, because that encourages other sucides. At one school the mother of a suicide wanted a page in the yearbook dedicated to her child, she wanted a moment of silence, she wanted a day of mourning, and she wanted to come to the school and talk to the kids about her son. The school called me up to ask if they should do all this, and I said, "Absolutely not!"

I don't believe in glorifying suicide because that encourages it. Suicide is bad behavior in its most extreme form, and bad behavior should not be glorified. If you make it a big deal then other lonely, hurting kids will think that if they commit suicide they'll get some attention, even if they aren't around to enjoy it. Cluster suicides are an example of glorifying the act. Kids as a group start dwelling on suicide and talking about it in an emotional, non-constructive manner. This is destructive; in effect they are glorifying death.

In my assembly I talk very little about suicide, and a lot about life. Depression is a fact of life. Everyone gets depressed. My underlying premise is that if you deal with depression on a rational, logical level you can prevent it and can teach kids how to recover from it.

I begin the *Dare to Live* program with the introduction at the beginning of this chapter. Next I show slides. Why slides? In the public schools, kids are pretty hard-core. The average American teenager has seen 18,000 violent deaths in 22,000 hours of television viewing, plus many more murders in the movie theater, by the time he or she is 18 years old. You get a distorted view of death when you see Charles Bronson in *Death Wish I, II, III* and *IV* blowing bad guys away one week, and a week later the bad guys are alive and well in another movie.

The reason for the slide show is so that students can identify with someone who was alive but is not alive anymore. The slides are of Paul Horne, a young man who committed suicide at not quite 16 years old in Clark County, Washington. The pictures the students see are included in the photos at the end of this book. Paul is not an exception. His is a very typical story.

Gresham Union High School

This is Paul when he was two. If you look closely you'll notice he is looking at his birthday cake. He is a typical two-year-old in that he is getting ready to wear it. Now my oldest daughter — she is in junior high school now — when she was a baby her favorite food was mashed potatoes and gravy. The way she would eat it is, you'd give her a spoon and she'd throw it on the floor. Then she would scoop up a handful of potatoes and she would wear them all over her face. Kids are disgusting. What can I say?

This is Paul when he was about three years of age. That's Paul in the middle with the football. He's pictured with two cousins that he spent a lot of time with as he grew up.

This is Paul with the same two cousins you saw in the earlier picture. He's in the middle, not looking too happy about having his picture taken.

Now this is Paul with the family dog. Paul wanted a pet, and he begged and begged until his father finally bought him a dog. The family still has the dog. It is a white cocker spaniel named Snowball, and it's a lot older and a lot fatter now.

This is Paul with his older sister at camp. (In the slide, Paul is riding a donkey.) Ugly, isn't she? Actually Paul didn't have any sisters. Paul would spend every summer at his grandfather's farm in Hawkinson, Washington. His grandfather bought this mule for the kids to ride. Paul was really close to his grandfather.

Another picture of his grandfather's farm. (Paul is sitting, beaming, on a tractor.)

This is Paul with his only brother, Wayne, who was two years older than Paul.

Paul again with his brother Wayne. They rebuilt the engine of this pickup truck together and were really proud of it.

Look at this picture. This is a cute picture. This is Paul at 12 years of age. Look at him. Typical 12-year-old: rumpled clothes, big cheesy grin, dirty hands, and a skinned-up nose.

Now look at the next picture, Paul at 13. What a change! You know what happened to him? Paul discovered girls. Nothing makes a guy comb his hair faster than discovering that girls do not carry the dreaded disease cooties.

This is Paul at Christmas. It was taken a few years ago. The Horne family's Christmas tradition is that they have the gift exchange early on Christmas morning and then have a large family breakfast. This picture was taken of Paul after the family's gift exchange and before breakfast.

This is a very interesting picture, because it is the last picture *taken of Paul Horne before he died. This was taken in August before he started his junior year at Fort Vancouver High School in Vancouver, Washington.*

Now, he went ahead and started his junior year at Fort Vancouver High School, and his first-period class was a health class. Mrs. Boggs, the instructor, had everyone write an essay in class on self-image. She had them title the essay, "Who Am I?"

In that essay Paul wrote that he thought himself to be extremely ugly. He actually thought he was the ugliest person who had ever lived. He said he didn't see any reason for living. He said that life at its best is a cruel hoax. He handed that essay in at the end of the period, and Mrs. Boggs read it during the day. She thought to herself, "This kid is really hurting. I need to talk to him." She couldn't find him the rest of that day, so she decided she'd talk to him the next day during first period.

But the next day Paul didn't come back to school. That night Paul wrote a letter to his brother, and in the letter he wrote: "Dear Wayne, if I stay here I'm just going to blow my brains out and that will hurt everybody. But I can't stand to keep living the way I am now. So I'm going to run away. And hopefully somewhere, somehow, I will find happiness. And if I do, I'll come home." He signed it, "Love, Paul," slid the note under his brother's door and left.

He packed a backpack, and he got about five miles from his home. He moved into an abandoned barn in the east part of Clark County. He stayed in the barn three or four days. One of the last things Paul Horne did was to take a .22 caliber pistol he had taken with him, take his driver's license out of his wallet and shoot his driver's license picture six times. Not the entire license, just the picture.

He then found a rope in the barn, made a noose, threw it over a rafter, stacked two boxes on top of each other, placed the noose around his neck and jumped off. Paul hung in that barn for five days before anybody discovered him.

As the chaplain of Clark County Fire District Five, I was called to the scene. It was my responsibility to go to scenes like that, to offer any kind of support that I could.

The deputy sheriff came up to me and said, "Mike, we found the young man's driver's license." That's when I saw how he'd shot his driver's license.

He said, "Would you go notify the parents?" That was my job.

I drove to the address on the driver's license and knocked on the door, and Mrs. Horne answered. I said, "Mrs. Horne, I'm Mike Miller. I'm the chaplain with the Fire Department."

She said, "It's about Paul, isn't it?"

I said, "Yes, it is."

She asked, "Is he all right?"

I said, "No, he's not."

Before I could say anything else she asked, "Is he in the hospital?"

I responded, "No, he's not, Mrs. Horne. Your son is dead." And I had to tell her that her son had taken his own life.

I went in the house and sat with her for four hours. During that four hours Mrs. Horne cried and cried and cried and cried, and she kept wanting the one thing I couldn't give her. The one thing I couldn't give her was her son.

And she kept asking me, "Why?" I couldn't give her an answer for that either.

It was while I was sitting in the living room of that home that I decided, "Mike, something has to be done."

2

What is Depression?

"Suicide is a permanent solution
to a temporary problem."
— Unknown

Depression

What is depression? What is this thing that would come and steal a person's life? For that matter, what brought 500,000 teenagers in the United States last year to the point where life was so unattractive that death became an option? When you're 13 or 16 or 19, there is everything to look forward to. There are games, dances, graduation, college, career, getting a car, marriage, having children, buying a home, and traveling. Teenagers have their whole lives ahead of them. What brings a person to the point that he or she no longer wants to live? To look at and to understand depression, it must be examined in its most basic, simple form.

Gresham Union High School

*B*ecoming depressed is exactly like catching a cold. When you catch a cold, it comes in stages. First you get what we call the sniffles. When you get the sniffles the worst thing that can happen is sitting in an English class taking a test, with the only sound in the room the scrape of the pencil on the paper, all of a sudden you develop . . . post-nasal drip.

You're sitting there in class, you're looking for a kleenex, and you don't have one. There is no noise, no one is talking, and finally you know you're going to drip on the test, and the teacher is going to frown on that. So you do the only thing left for you to do. You do this: Sniffffff.

Everyone else is wondering, "Did he swallow it?" Now don't think I'm being gross, because every one of you has thought about it at one time or another.

You ever see a little kid, two years old? You know, I've got four kids, and when they get runny noses they just don't care. If they've got it coming out one side or the other, it just doesn't matter.

But no one ever died of the sniffles. You'll never see a doctor's report that says, "The patient was admitted to the emergency room at 6 a.m. He died at 10 a.m. because his nose ran to death." It doesn't happen. But what happens if you don't treat the sniffles? What happens is that it turns into a head cold.

You come downstairs and your mom says, "How are you?"

You say, "I feel awful."

She looks at you and says, "Well, maybe you'd better stay home from school today."

For a moment you say, "Oh, good idea," but then you realize that it's Friday and if you stay home from school she's not going to let you go out tonight. You say, "No, I'm fine." You grab a Contac and away you go.

So you're running around and you're pushing yourself. You go to the game and go out afterwards. You're running around, you're not getting the sleep, the food, the rest, the nutrients, the vitamins *you need, all the stuff your body craves. You're just running around, and the cold gets worse.*

No one has ever died of the sniffles. But gradually the cold gets worse and worse and worse to the point that you have pneumonia, and lots of people die of pneumonia. No one dies up here. (Points to nose.) Lots of people die down here. (Points to chest.)

Depression works exactly the same way.

Depression is gloominess, sadness, or dejection. People say they're "feeling down" or "feeling bad." How often have you heard people casually say they feel "depressed" about their job prospects, wardrobe, or checkbook balance? But real depression is a larger, deeper hurt. Depression is an emotional heartache.

As adults, most of us do not need depression explicitly defined, for we have lived through any number of rounds of it. We are able to deal with depression more easily than teens because adults are generally considered emotionally mature. Yet even with a maturity advantage, every year thousands of adults seek counseling, have nervous breakdowns, or commit suicide because of depression that is not treated. How much more confusing is it for young people who have never dealt with depression? Not only do they feel bad, sad, and hopeless, but they aren't sure how they arrived at that state or if they will ever find their way out of it. They don't realize that depression will pass.

To teenagers, depression is a comment on their mental health. It worries them because they feel mentally unstable. "I must be nuts," they say to themselves as they become more depressed. They're sure of it when they start having suicidal feelings. On top of that they feel the pressure of conformity. Teenagers want to be accepted above all else. The last thing they want is to be different, and being mentally ill would certainly make them different. They understand that they are feeling badly, but they don't know how to label what they are experiencing.

Teenagers need to understand that they are experiencing depression, that it's a normal part of life, and that depression is an emotional state, not a mental illness.

Once depression deepens and teenagers decide — mistakenly — that they are mentally ill, they usually don't seek help. They don't tell anyone how they are feeling. And just like a common cold that is left untreated, the depression gets worse.

Learning About Depression

Teenagers are children in transition. They need to learn about depression and how to deal with it, just as they learned spelling and math. It is hard for parents to remember this, because teens may look physically mature and yet be emotionally immature. That six-foot-tall, 180-pound Hercules who bears your son's name has a birth certificate that says he is 17 years old. But he may feel and act 10 years old emotionally. The four aspects — mental, physical, spiritual, and emotional — mature at different rates. As with a strapping 17-year-old, physical maturity often comes before emotional, mental, and spiritual maturity.

The most powerful method that parents have to help their children through depression is to tell them that it is O.K. to hurt and to teach them how to deal with the pain they will experience. Often kids turn to drugs or alcohol because they don't understand what is wrong or how to fix it, and chemical highs temporarily ease the emotional pain.

It is important for teens to know that *depression has a beginning, a middle, and an end.* Coming out of depression can take just as long as entering it. What has taken months to build will take weeks, maybe even months, to heal. Realizing that one is depressed, and why, opens the door to recovery. If I may borrow an example from the Gresham Union High School program, a diagnosis of pneumonia is often the first step toward feeling better. Even if you still feel physically like death warmed over, you feel emotionally relieved. ("Something was wrong after all!") Just knowing that depressed feelings will eventually pass is the beginning of recuperation.

Young people who are emotionally immature — or, better yet, emotionally growing — are impatient for results. Once they understand that they are experiencing depression and that it will end, they want instant recovery. In this age of microwaves, fast food, and jet airplanes it is easy to get discouraged if we don't feel better immediately. I tell students that life is a series of experiences; there are no instant answers. Becoming depressed is a gradual process, and it takes a gradual process to recover from depression.

Bad Days

One cause of depression is the bad day, or what I call the "emotional cold." Certainly everyone has bad days, and when they happen once in a while they are as harmless as the sniffles. But when a bad day follows one bad day upon another bad day, depression takes a strong hold on a person's emotions. Certainly an occasional bad day will not kill anyone, but a pileup of bad days, leading to depression and suicidal feelings, kills thousands every year.

For a teenager, a bad day can be caused by a number of things. Teens are changing more rapidly than they did even as young children. Not only are they changing hormonally, causing rapid physical changes, but they are also striving to grow emotionally, mentally, and spiritually. They are like a pendulum swinging from one extreme to another. They are discovering new ideas, new feelings, and new attitudes. But they still want to be taken care of and nurtured.

Teenagers feel driven to search for their own ideals, heroes, and thoughts. Teens are looking for their own identities and taking the first steps toward adult responsibility. They want to assert their individuality. If mom and dad believe in anything, that thing is suspect. But young people still look up to their folks and come to them for advice. This mix of child and adult emotions, maturity and immaturity, makes everything a big deal.

New experiences cause bad days. It is hard for adults to remember that what seems old hat to them — a kiss, a date (or the lack of a date), a failing grade, or flunking a driving test — are first-time experiences for the adolescent. This gives these things an importance and a significance that adults tend to overlook.

Lack of success, another first for many young people, also plays a large role in teenage depression. Failing is never easy, and if you've never done it before, it takes a big emotional toll. Compound a few bad days with intense first-time experiences and confusion about growing up, and it is no wonder that one hundred percent of teenagers feel depressed at one point or another.

Pressures Behind Depression

Depression didn't start with the current generation of teenagers, nor will it end even when teens and adults understand what it is. Depression is a by-product of a changing and confusing society. We live in a high-pressure world, and teenagers, and younger children as well, are very much aware of these pressures.

Parental pressure is one of the most common and harmful pressures with which all young people live. Often we don't realize how much we are pressuring our kids, even as we do it. We want our children to succeed and if possible to do better in life than we have. We expect them to stand out in school, excel in sports, or shine in the arts. It is not wrong to expect children to do their best, but many parents lose sight of the person they are raising and look only at the awards the student has or has not received.

We can teach kids to work hard without teaching that perfection is the only acceptable result. Being a good sportsman and enjoying sports are more important than winning or being the best player on the team. Having a well-rounded education and a love of learning is better than being unable to take risks because of fear of failure. Parents do not need to add the pressure of high expectations to their children's daily stress in simply making it through school.

Teenagers pick up parents' expectations and then act as their own worst critics. They want to succeed in order to please mom and dad, but they may already be working at their maximum capacities. When they disappoint their parents, or when they *think* they'll disappoint their parents, kids get discouraged and depressed. They should always be praised for successes, however small, rather than scolded for not living up to their parents' possibly unrealistic hopes. Most kids are harder on themselves than adults ever dream of being.

Seventeen-year-old Jennifer committed suicide on the first day of her senior year. She was an "A" student, captain of the track team, and had been a beautiful homecoming princess the year before. Jennifer was pretty and popular, but she came to the conclusion that life was not worth living. She could not handle the pressure of being "perfect" any longer.

By anyone's measure, this teenager was a success. But the cost of success was her life. The fears Jennifer kept inside about school and failing, fears she couldn't deal with, led her to commit suicide at the beginning of a year that held the promises of her future. When will the pressures stop? Who will teach teenagers that it is O.K. to be second-best or average if they are doing all they can?

School is a source of pressure because it often pits student against student. We live in a very competitive society, and competition is built into the school system. We like to reward "the best." Less than the best is nothing. We emphasize winning and losing, starting with such seemingly innocent events as Spelling Bees and Field Days. In a Spelling Bee, one out of 30 children will be the winner. All the rest will label themselves losers. Field Days are supposed to be end-of-the-school-year celebrations. But when you give out ribbons for the winners and nothing for the losers, these events can make the school year end painfully for a majority of kids. Competition in small doses is healthy, but too often competition is overemphasized, and our children suffer.

Children are thrown into a pressure cooker at school in other ways as well. For example, in third grade they are expected to learn multiplication tables. Not only must they learn all the tables in a prescribed length of time, but they must also perform on command by spitting back the information within a specified time limit. Children feel the pressure of this task, especially if they are among the last to accomplish it. Multiplication tables are important, and children can and do learn them, but the pressure adds to their sense of helplessness. School is necessary, but it's not often easy.

The way in which we teach can also increase pressure on students. In many classrooms teachers are supposed to grade on a curve, which means someone will get an "A" but someone else will fall under the curve and flunk. Rarely are teachers allowed to grade on improvement shown or take into account different learning styles. Yet we want educators to teach our children *and* understand their differences. This is an unrealistic expectation to place on the schools. This system forces many students constantly to struggle to reach standard achievement measures that don't consider individuality.

With today's emphasis on careers and "making it to the top," students are feeling pressured into life decisions earlier and earlier: "What college will I attend? What career will I pursue?" Thus we make them grow up faster — often faster than they are able. Most teens can't decide what to wear in the morning, let alone what job they want to hold for the rest of their lives. (For that matter, most adults don't know what they want to be "when they grow up" either.) Twelve-, 14-, 16-, and even 18-year-olds need freedom to explore many different careers and life options without being expected to stick forever to any one "career" decision.

The pressure of emphasizing school over everything else harms our kids. What happens when you emphasize the mental growth of maturing human beings without providing equal nurturing for their spiritual and emotional needs? You produce unhappy, hurting children. If we overemphasize test scores, grades, and getting into an elite university, we do so at the expense of personal growth. Young people need to learn how to deal with disappointment and failure along with learning good study habits.

School not only brings to bear the stresses of academics, but also the intense drive to be liked and accepted by one's school-mates. Because kids are willing to make almost any sacrifice to find acceptance, peer pressure can cost: it is directly related to drug use and alcohol consumption by teenagers. We can blame peer influence for early sexual activity and shoplifting, too. ("I'll do it if you'll do it. Come on, I dare you!")

One reason for the popularity of gangs in inner cities is that a gang provides kids who have little other support with a group that accepts them. Even when the group's activities are illegal or immoral, young people and adults join because the gang offers a place where they can belong, where they are accepted.

Peer pressure is felt on a group level as well as on an individual level. Every high school demonstrates this with a unique social climate. As I go from school to school, it is obvious what is "in" at each community. At one school it is socially acceptable to be punks. At another, everyone dresses like cowboys, and at a third, all the kids look like preppies. Each school has a dress and behavior code that is accepted by students as the norm.

The results of group peer pressure can be dramatic. If the most popular students are drug users and say that drug use is cool, then everyone believes it and drug use becomes rampant. At my high school in Detroit, it was death to your popularity to be a virgin past your thirteenth birthday. That is peer group pressure.

People generally fall into two groups: leaders and followers. The vast majority are followers. Peer pressure certainly can be responsible for setting positive examples, as with Students Against Drunk Driving and peer counseling groups. But problems arise when the leaders do things that are harmful — using drugs, drinking, or promoting casual sex, to name a few — because the followers follow. In some areas, entire neighborhoods and cities fall under the spell of strong leaders who support immorality.

Students quickly learn that to be different from the group means ostracism by a large portion of the student body. And no matter who you are, rejection hurts. Conforming to peer pressure is one way to protect oneself against rejection.

No matter how tough teenagers look or act — and gang members, punks, and bikers can look pretty hardened — they are not tough inside. On the inside they are crying out for love and acceptance. Teens are confused by the changes they are going through, by the fluctuation of their feelings, by the pressures from parents, school, and peers, and by their struggle to deal with all of this. Social and personal pressures chip away at their lives, and too often depression is the result.

Susan

Fourteen-year-old Susan came to see me after a *Dare to Live* program at her school. Her parents were divorced. She lived with her dad and had not seen her mother in years. "My father doesn't understand me," Susan began.

"Do you ever try talking to him?" I asked.

"No, he won't listen to me. He only wants to think I'm

sweet and innocent, and a perfect, obedient child. I'm not. I sneak out every Friday and Saturday night. I drink, I sleep with guys, and I use drugs."

Susan then looked at me and asked, "What do you think of me now?"

"Does it matter what I think?"

"Yes," she said, "it does."

"I think you're a little girl who is hurting," I answered. "I think you've done things that you wish you hadn't. I think you are still doing things that you wish you didn't have to do. But you're doing them because you have to be accepted. I want you to know that I accept you the way you are, and I care."

Susan's eyes filled with tears. "No one has ever said that to me before."

If children are not told that they are loved and lovable no matter what they do, they will constantly test the boundaries. Susan's life was a desert with no love in sight. She had no evidence that her mother loved her; she had not seen her for seven years. Her father's love was based on an image of her being a "perfect," obedient child, which was something Susan knew that she was not and could not be. Susan looked for acceptance from the only group that seemed to give her the unconditional love she craved: her peers. Because of her desire to be accepted, she participated in things she knew were wrong.

Social Pressures

In addition to pressures from parents, school, and peers, teenagers are very much aware of the changing social climate and the uncertainties of life on this planet.

Since the 1940s social changes have accelerated phenomenally. During World War II women began working outside the home and found that they liked it. Then the economy changed, and women worked outside the home, not only because it was satisfying, but because it became a necessity. In many parts of the United States it is difficult for a family to live on one income.

Some psychologists believe that the price our children pay for absentee parents is high. In this society there is less parenting and supervision of young children than ever before. After having paid childcare costs for seven or eight years, parents decide their first- or second-graders are able to supervise themselves for the three or four hours before mom and dad come home from work. The number of latchkey kids is growing in spite of laws that prohibit young children from being without adult supervision.

Kids with no supervision exist in a vacuum without adult love and support. Children want and need a loving and safe environment and are unlikely to find it in an empty house after school. Without adults to guide them, lonely kids turn to the next closest source — usually friends — for love and acceptance. Parents may work out of necessity, but by their absenteeism they give away the responsibility of teaching their children about issues that were meant to be taught at home. Some parents expect the schools, or maybe even the child's peers, to teach the child about sex, morality, and ethics. That is when social climates at school and in the neighborhood become the key to what children learn and how they act.

Families have changed as society has changed. Many teenagers now belong to families that have gone through three generations of divorce. It's no wonder that teens worry about their parents' marriage. Grandma and grandpa, as well as mom and dad, are divorced. With the addition of stepparents and stepsiblings the family unit becomes more complex. Divorces and remarriages do not necessarily cause problems or depression, but they do add stress.

The mobility of American families makes home life even more unsettled. Americans now average 11 moves per lifetime, according to the Census Bureau. They move out of school districts, neighborhoods, cities, and states. It is not unusual for an average-size school to get one hundred transfers, either in or out, during the first three months of the school year. As a result, teens do not have the stability that can be found in a friend they have known for five years, two years, or even just one year. A teen's best friend may be someone they met a few months ago, not someone they've known since fourth grade. And the odds are that one of the two will move away within the next few years.

Then world problems come crashing in on the already fragile teenager. The threats of nuclear war, an unstable economy, AIDS, and a host of other crises make the headlines daily. Teens not only have to worry about whether they will get a date on Friday night, but, if they do get a date and are sexually active, whether they will catch a disease and die. Young people are well aware of society's many problems, and these worries add to their other pressures. For teens today, the Earth often seems an unstable place in which to live.

A Universal Experience

In a high school survey that I did, I asked the students questions about depression. Of the kids who returned the survey, one hundred percent said they had been depressed. But only 14 percent thought that other people got depressed too. Nearly all the kids believed that depression was unique to them. Kids don't realize that *all* their fellow high school and junior high classmates at one time have been and at some time again will be depressed. In an auditorium full of students, every one of them raise their hands when asked if they have experienced depression. As the students look around the room, they realize that without exception the cheerleaders, the athletes, the student-body president, and even the teachers have experi-

sometimes feel down, it must be all right and even "normal" to be depressed. And it is!

For those who are convinced that being different is the worst way to be, knowing that everyone else suffers in the same way is important. Teenagers who understand that we all hurt and all become depressed no longer have to fear depression. They also don't have to feel uncomfortable seeking help when they need it.

No-Fault Clause

It is not surprising that as children become adolescents and begin to cope with social changes and the pressures of becoming an adult, they become depressed. But I want to emphasize that a depressed teenager is not a reflection on his or her parents.

Teens do not get depressed because their parents have missed something. Whether or not you have heart-to-heart talks with your kids every night, read all the right parenting manuals, are open and have great communication skills, your children will still experience depression. No matter what kind of home they come from, kids will experience emotional ups and downs. Parents cannot and should not try to protect their children from the highs and the lows. Both have to be experienced, because we learn different aspects of life from both.

Communication

The best therapy for depression is to deal with the source of the pain. What caused the hurt in the first place? This takes communication, and many teenagers don't know how to open up and talk. They especially don't know how to communicate pain.

Communication skills are learned. Effective communication between parent and child should be practiced from the beginning. When eight-year-old Jeff wants to share his fears about second grade with mom, she should give him the same respect she would give an adult friend who came to her with a problem. But instead Jeff's mom smooths over the problem: "It will work out, don't worry about it." Or she ignores it: "I'm busy, Jeff, and you complain too much anyway." This tells Jeff that his problems are not important enough to bother mom about them.

After five more years of having his problems minimized or ignored, Jeff, now 13, no longer tries to talk to his parents about his concerns. His typical reaction when he has a problem and is hurting is, "My parents don't listen anyway." Unfortunately, the pattern that began many years before confirms this for Jeff.

Kids who are hurting inside have difficulty reaching out for help, and will often quit reaching out if their early attempts are unsuccessful. They learn this technique from their parents. Adults close up when they don't want to talk about a problem: "Nothing is wrong. Leave me alone. I don't feel like talking." It is not surprising that teens also withdraw when they are depressed. The problem is that nothing gets resolved by withdrawal. Depression deepens when it is not discussed.

Communicating with children, giving them respect, and paying attention to their problems and successes must begin early. But even if negative patterns have developed, it is never too late to change. Parents must be honest about their failings: "I know in the past I haven't been a very good listener, but I would really like to try harder. I want you to know that I'm here for you whether you are happy or hurting. I will do my best to listen to you without judgment."

It may be hard to regain the trust of children who have not seen evidence of their parents' sincerity and change of heart. But all kids want their parents to be there for them. If you give them reason to believe you will support them by being available during small crises, they will begin to share larger problems with you as well.

Remember, communication is important *before* your children become depressed. Shutting kids out, minimizing their problems, and being unavailable when they need you makes it unlikely that they will come to you when they hurt. Being open, honest, and nonjudgmental, listening for subtle clues about their emotional states, and being available to them in large and small ways keeps the lines of communication between parent and child open and uncluttered.

Sources of Support

Depressed adolescents are hurting. They want the hurt to stop but don't know how to stop it. The reasons for their pain are varied and may come from the circumstances of their lives or from the pressures visited upon them by parents, peers, school, or society. But what they all need in common is support to get through the tough times.

If the adults in their lives are absent or are not willing to support them, teenagers will turn to friends for advice. But friends are usually not trained or experienced in dealing with depression. Their advice may be to mask the problem, deny it, or ignore it.

Often, friends will givel the hurting teen what they believe is an instant solution: "If you feel bad, take drugs. Get drunk. Run away from home." But if young people cover depression with drugs and alcohol, how can they know what they are feeling? It is impossible to know how you feel or how to make yourself feel better in an alcohol- or drug-induced state.

Running away from home appears to be another quick and easy solution. If kids can't talk to their parents, they reason, their parents must be the problem. So they leave. Most runaways quickly learn that life outside the home is more complex and frightening than facing mom and dad and their own difficulties.

Why do friends pass out this kind of advice? Kids are not

taught how to deal with their own depression, so they therefore know even less about dealing with a friend's depression. But if there is no other support, it is friends to whom the depressed teenager will go for help.

Young adults must be taught where to turn for reliable, wise support. If they do not have the built-in support of families and a network of support from well-informed friends, counselors, church, and community leaders, we need to teach them to care for each other. If depressed teens can reach out to friends who know how to help, they will not feel so alone in the world.

At a high school in Seattle, Washington, a group of teens gathered around me after the *Dare to Live* program. I noticed a girl who held back as other students commented on my stories or asked for advice for a friend. Finally, two girls remained. The young woman who had held back was named Jolene; she told the other girl, Beth, that she could speak first.

Beth told me a life story of tragic proportions. Her parents were divorced, and Beth lived with her mom. Her mother's boyfriend appeared when the welfare check came and disappeared with the money. There was no food in the house, and Beth's little brother often went to school without a lunch or lunch money. Beth had been babysitting to give her little brother money for lunch, but she recently discovered that an older brother had been stealing from the younger child to buy drugs. Fifteen-year-old Beth was overwhelmed with the responsibilities of acting as a surrogate parent to her younger brother and of trying to make it through her own mixed-up life.

Jolene listened to Beth's story and realized that she was not the only person who hurt. At that point Jolene was willing to share her similarly sad story with Beth and me. The two girls, who had never met before, agreed to become each other's support system. They promised to look for the other at school every day and to check on how each was doing. These two hurting teenagers began the framework of support they both needed to face their problems.

Teenagers are relieved to learn that it is all right to offer support to each other. When I ask at a *Dare to Live* assembly how many students would be willing to reach out to a fellow student who needs help, every hand eagerly raises. Hurting kids realize that they are not alone in their fear and suffering. If they are told it is O.K. to talk about depression and suicide to their friends, and these friends learn how to listen and how to seek outside help if necessary, troubles are brought out into the open. A common misconception is that talking about depression and suicide *creates* problems. That just isn't true. Encouraging young people to talk about how they feel *solves* problems. Kids talking to kids builds support.

It is important to have more than one person to whom turn in times of need. A support system must be deep, made up of many people who are willing to help. It is impossible to have too much support. Everyone — both young people and adults — should constantly be building support systems.

During a *Dare to Live* assembly I call six kids up front to represent the different places that teens can go to find help when they are feeling bad: their family, friends, school, community workers, community programs, and professionals in the mental health field. I also ask the teachers to reinforce this point in the classroom, and I encourage them to have their students compile personal lists of support people. In the Appendix of this book is a sheet that readers may use for the same purpose. Tear it out or photocopy it and give it to a teen about whom you care. This will become a personal list of the teen's support system that will be available should it be needed.

Depression is a negative state, but it can be dealt with in a positive manner when we provide each other with support. We must care for one another. True, "no man is an island," but it seems that as the world gets more populated, people become more isolated. Relationships, the foundation of support, must be built in the old-fashioned way: I care about you, so you'll care about me, so we can care about each other.

Scott

Other emotions besides depression are being experienced for the first time during adolescence. Kids need to be taught about these emotions, too.

Take 15-year-old Scott, who listened to the program and approached me afterwards. Scott was worried that he was depressed.

"I do eight of those 12 signs," he told me.

Over the years I've learned to spot kids who are feeling bad, and Scott didn't look depressed to me. "What kinds of problems are you having?" I asked. "Are you doing O.K. at home?"

"Yeah," Scott said.

"Are you doing O.K. at school?"

"Yeah, I'm doing fine at school."

"What seems to be the problem?" I said.

"Well, I'm having trouble sleeping. I can't concentrate in class. My stomach is all knotted up and I don't feel like eating."

"How long have you felt this way?" I said.

Scott thought for a minute. "About a month."

"Was there anything different that happened a month ago, Scott?"

He looked puzzled. "I met Lisa."

Scott wasn't depressed! He was in love for the first time, and he didn't know that his confused feelings might stem from an emotion that was supposed to be wonderful. Teenagers must be told about the whole range of emotions they will experience, from depression to love.

Success

Which kids succeed? The students who are truly successful are not free of depression. *Everyone experiences depression. It is a normal, healthy emotion.* But success is more likely when teens have a network of support, when they know how to communicate, and when they know their parents, or someone else, will listen to them.

Successful teenagers are taught that it is all right not to be perfect and that failure is not only acceptable, but to be expected. These kids work out problems more promptly. Although they go through their share of emotional upheavals, they have the knowledge and the support to deal with difficulties as they occur.

Gresham Union High School

I'm not talking to you about something I've read in books; I've actually lived through this. About five years ago I developed migraine headaches and a shaking in my hand. I went to a neurologist to find out what was wrong with me.

He ran about $2,000 worth of tests and said, "Well, Mike, I've got good news and I've got bad news."

I said, "What's the good news?"

He said, "I can't find anything wrong with you."

"What's the bad news?"

"There's something wrong with you."

"For $2,000 you're telling me that?"

"What you've got, Mike, is an acentral tremor. Now, we don't know what causes it, but it can be treated."

I said, "Well, how do you treat it?"

"We treat it with medication. I'm going to give you medication and I want you to take it for a month. Come back so I can see how you're doing."

I took the medication. I came back in a month and he said, "How are you doing?"

I said, "Fine," but not with much enthusiasm.

"What's wrong?"

"Nothing."

"Headaches?"

"No, I haven't had a headache all month."

"Shaking?"

"No shaking."

"What's wrong?"

"It's kind of embarrassing."

"Come on. I'm your doctor, tell me."

"Doc, ever since I started taking that stuff, I've lost my sex drive."

"That's not good."

"You're telling me! My wife's got me sleeping on the couch!"

"It's a side effect of the medication. Various medications have different side effects for different people. I'll change your prescription and put you on Corgard. Come back in a month and let me know how you're doing."

So I started taking Corgard. I went back in a month, and he asked again, *"How are you doing?"*

I said, *"Great! No headaches, no shaking, my sex drive is back to normal. Good stuff!"*

He said, *"Fine. Take it for six months and come back and let me see how you're doing."*

He forgot to mention one small detail — that some people who take Corgard develop deep, deep depression as a side effect. Now, you realize that depression builds. I didn't take one Corgard and say, *"Oh no, I'm depressed."* But after five months I was full-blown depressed. I was hurting so much I didn't know what was going on. It was awful.

I hurt so bad I decided I was going to do something I had never done before in my entire life: I was going to get drunk. I'd been to junior high, high school, college, Navy. I'd been around a lot of people who drank. I never drank. I never wanted to drink.

When I was a high school sophomore I went to a football game and the party afterward. A football player walked up to me and said, *"Here Miller, have a beer."* I took it because I was afraid he wouldn't like me if I didn't.

I stood there holding the beer thinking, "I'm baaad." Then I *smelled it. Uhggggg. You know what it looks like, don't you? Yeah, it foams like it too. I'm standing there with this beer in my hands and I don't want to drink it, because if it smells like that, and it looks like that, it's probably going to taste like that. I didn't want to find out.*

But pretty soon I realized that if I didn't drink this, people were going to laugh at me and were going to see that I was not drinking. So inspiration struck. I took the can of beer and brought it up to my mouth. I stuck my tongue in the hole, tipped the can back and went "gulp, gulp, gulp," brought it down, threw the still-full can in the bushes and said, "Give me another brewski!" Not a drop went in my mouth.

Mike Miller, sophomore, 15 years of age — I developed a reputation that night. I was the first human being in history who could drink 24 cans of beer and never go to the bathroom. Everyone thought I had a bladder as big as a basketball. I didn't know that the stuff went right through you.

But until I was depressed I had never gotten drunk, never wanted to. Kids used to come up to me and say, "Miller, let's go get drunk."

I'd say, "Why?"

"Well, it's Friday."

"So?"

"We're teenagers; we're supposed to."

"What do you mean we're supposed to? You guys go out, you get drunk, and you throw up on each other in the car. That doesn't sound like much fun. If you want to get sick, my mom made a tuna noodle casserole that went bad. We could go eat that and get just as sick."

But this particular day I was hurting so bad I was willing to try anything to feel better. I drove to a liquor store and walked in. I'd never been in a liquor store. It's wall-to-wall bottles. I didn't know there were so many ways to get drunk.

The clerk came up to me and asked, "May I help you?"

"Yeah, give me some of that clear stuff."

"What size?"

"I don't know," I said, "give me a quart."
"I think a pint will be enough."
"That's all right. Give me a pint."
So he sold me a pint. I went out to my car. I didn't even know what I'd purchased. I pulled it out of the bag and looked at it. IT was 120-proof Smirnoff vodka.

I unscrewed the lid and smelled it, and I went, "Oooooh!" I thought beer smelled bad! This was worse! Then I put my tongue down into the neck of the bottle and splashed a little up onto my tongue, and I went, "Ack, uggg, gross."

So I went to the grocery store and bought a quart of orange juice. I drove down to the park and poured half the orange juice out, poured the vodka into the quart container and mixed it up.

I sat there in the front seat of my car, about 10:30 in the morning, thinking, "How much of this will I have to drink to be drunk?" You see, there was no expert there. No one to say, "You're stewed. You're ploughed. You're blotto." So I thought about it and remembered that people who were drunk could no longer talk straight. I decided that when I could no longer say "Peter Piper picked a peck of pickled peppers," I'd know I was drunk.

So I took a gulp. I forgot to tell you that I hadn't eaten in two days. I took a gulp and what I did next was totally involuntary. I did this: "Gagg, ug, ack."

On this particular day there was no one to impress, so every time I'd take a drink I'd gag and go, "Peter Piper picked a peck of pickled peppers."

Gulp. "Peter Piper picked a peck of pickled peppers."

Gulp. "Peter Piper picked a peck of pickled peppers. This stuff isn't working." I was drinking that fast.

Gulp. "Peter Piper picked a peck of pickled peppers."

Gulp. "Mbxibodkwwk." My tongue grew hair. I had fur growing from the roof of my mouth. I drank that entire quart of orange juice and vodka in 50 minutes. It was now a little after 11 in the morning, I'm sitting in the front seat of my car trying desperately to get my eyeballs to focus, and I'm watching the trees walk by.

The trees are doing this (waves hand through the air). The clouds are doing this (waves hand the other direction), and my stomach is doing this (boogies). About that time my stomach called up to my brain. You know what I'm talking about, when the stomach goes, "Um, brain. This is the stomach talking."

And the brain says, "Uh, right, stomach, what do you want?"

"Uh, we're getting ready to barf down here, big time."

So you know I'm thinking, "Hey, Mike, if you're going to throw up, you're going to get up and go to the bathroom. You're going to throw up in a toilet like any decent civilized human being would do."

So my brain calls down to my legs, "Legs, let's get up and walk over to the bathroom."

My legs call back, "Ain't no way."

And my stomach starts, "Ten, nine, eight, seven . . . ."

Here I was getting ready to ralph on my dashboard. What I did was open the car door, stumble out and try to crawl to the bathroom. I got grass stains on my nose. I got dirt in my teeth. I left a foamy orange trail behind me.

And I'm glad none of you were there, because I can see how much sympathy I would have gotten.

The next four hours of my life were totally miserable. It was open the car door, throw up, close the car door. Open the car door, throw up, until finally my body got what is called the dry heaves. Enough said about that.

But you take a 30-year-old man who is already depressed and put that much alcohol into his system, and three things take place. One, he gets drunk. Two, he gets sick. And number three, he gets more depressed than he was when he started, because alcohol is a drug. It is a depressant. What it did was push me deeper into the depression that I was already feeling.

Questions and Answers

At the end of each chapter I will answer typical questions I field from parents and teenagers. These questions address specific issues about each chapter's topic.

1. Is depression a mental illness?

Depression is not a mental illness, but it can be an emotional or physical illness. I look at emotional needs as a continuum of feelings, with depression on one end and love at the other end of the scale. Sometimes the scale tips toward depression, other times toward happiness or love. There are also physical reasons people become depressed, including problems with a chemical imbalance, diseases like diabetes, or drug and alcohol use.

2. What's the difference between clinical and emotional depression?

Clinical depression is brought on by a physical problem, such as a reaction to a drug or a hormonal imbalance. Clinical depression involves a biological reason for depression. Emotional depression develops because of circumstances in someone's life — bad days, for example — that bring one to the point of depression.

3. Is depression more likely at certain ages?

No. Everyone can become depressed, young or old. Parents need to realize that even very little children can and will get depressed. More kids get depressed during adolescence because it is a time of intense change and turbulence. But anyone, at any age, can get depressed.

4. Do girls get depressed more often than boys?

No. What I see is that girls tend to be more outwardly emotional, but the fact that most boys hide their turmoil doesn't mean that they aren't depressed. Girls may be more vocal, more apt to cry, and more likely to let the sad feelings out. Boys say, "Guys don't cry," and they try to hide what they are going through. Girls and boys both get depressed, but girls are more likely to let the symptoms show.

5. Is depression contagious, genetic, or more likely in certain families?

Yes, in a sense it is contagious. It can seem contagious because if one kid hurts and the people around him care, when they see that hurt they start hurting too. This happens especially among young people. Let's say a teen is being, or has been, sexually molested and is very hurt. When the victim tells his or her best friend, that friend cannot change what has happened, and they've been sworn to secrecy so they can't share the problem either. The friend now hurts badly, too. They may even react as Stacie did. Stacie's suicide was a result of her caring for a friend who was hurting and then suffering rejection on top of that pain. You might also call depression contagious or genetic if you're talking about a physical reason for depression.

Another possibility is that depression within a family is a learned behavior. We can certainly learn from our parents to be pessimistic or optimistic. In some families young people learn how *not* to handle pressure. If children see their parents not dealing well with pressure and subsequent depression, they won't learn how to handle depression themselves either.

6. If my child is depressed, should I leave him alone?

Look at it this way. If your children are sick, do you leave them alone to get better all by themselves? If kids are depressed, don't ignore it or say, "They'll work it out," and leave them alone. Let them know that you care, that you're concerned, and that you understand what they're going through. Take whatever steps the teen will allow at the time, depending on how they feel. Whether they are a little depressed or a lot depressed, minister to them according to their needs.

7. Have things really changed that much since I was a teen? What are these kids experiencing that we didn't?

There is a twofold reason for increased teenage depression and suicide. First, the pressures of life have increased: world economic fluctuations, AIDS, nuclear weaponry, Third World starvation, war, pollution, and other crises are in the news constantly. Kids see and hear a lot about these issues, so there is a lot more stress than there was 50 or even 20 years ago.

Second, there has been a breakdown of the "traditional" family, which means less support for kids during these more troubled times. Families also move more frequently, so kids lose close friends, too. Long-term support has eroded in our society. Kids hurt and don't know where to turn for help.

8. Can you give too much support to kids?

I don't think so, and if I'm going to make the mistake of giving too much or too little help, I'd rather err on the side of too much. If you give too much help the teen will finally say, "Mom, dad, leave me alone!" But if you don't give enough, they will not say, "Hey, I need more help." If you're going to choose one way or the other, I'd say go with too much help.

9. How do I start talking to my children about depression?

First, I'd recommend talking before they become depressed. Parents must say to their kids, "Look, there are times when you're going to have bad days. You're going to get depressed. You're going to have your heart broken and your best friend is probably going to move away." If you tell kids that these hard emotional experiences are to be expected and are part of life, they'll be better able to handle them.

You're not trying to break them down or bum them out; you are saying that if it happens to them you will understand, it will be O.K. to cry, and you will be there to talk about it. Then when kids go through the tough times, they won't be confused by how they feel. They'll remember and say, "Gosh, if mom and dad understood this might happen, maybe I can go to them."

10. Am I qualified to deal with this? Won't I make it worse if I talk to my kids about their problems?

As far as being qualified, you're the parent. You should be the first person to whom they turn for help. Who is better qualified than someone who loves the child as much as you do?

And if you love your teenager, let them know it's all right to hurt. Give them hugs and spend time just listening to them. Don't try to have the answers, just listen and let them vent their feelings, because you care. You're not going to find anyone who cares for your child more than you do, and that makes you the most qualified for the job.

But know your limits. Again, let's look at it like a physical illness. If your child says they have a tummy ache, you don't rush them to the doctor. You do what you can do to help first. But if the child gets sicker, or if you feel that the problem is beyond your expertise, you take them to a professional. Use common sense. If you do everything you can to help your teenager overcome a bout of depression, but it is more than you feel qualified to handle, by all means take him or her to a professional.

3

Twelve Warning Signs

"It is characteristic of wisdom
not to do desperate things."
— Henry David Thoreau

Gresham Union High School

Depression starts out with what we call the "bad day." Ever had a bad day? You know what I'm talking about. Let's consider the young ladies first. Young ladies, have you ever been home on Friday night, no date, no one's coming over, nowhere to go, and you walk into the bathroom and in 37 seconds make your hair look exactly the way you've always wanted it to look?

Every hair falls into place. You put your makeup on and it flows. You stagger back from the mirror and say, "I look maaaahvelous!" But the only person who's home is your little brother, and he thinks you're a dog all the time.

But let's say it's something important, like picture day at school. This is the day they take your picture and put it in the yearbook for all time and eternity, and you want to look good. So you get up at three in the morning. You wash your hair, you dry your hair, you

55

comb your hair, you brush your hair, you frizz it, you fry it, you perm it, you take it off, you put it back on—all the things that young women do to their hair to make it look as nice as it does. But the longer you work, the worse it looks.

You have this one curl that sticks straight up at the side. After two hours, a quart of hair spray, and a tube of vaseline, you get that sucker to lie flat. You walk outside. The wind blows. Boiinng! Not only does it stick out, but it's as hard as a rock and it's considered a lethal weapon in most states. You show up at school and your friends want to know when you went punk. That is having a bad day.

Guys have bad days too. Isn't that true? When I was in eighth grade I was waiting to get my picture taken. There were two young ladies in front of me, and I was eavesdropping. Now ladies, let me tell you something. Guys eavesdrop on girls' conversations all the time. They do! They act like "we don't really care," but they are listening all the time.

These two young ladies were talking, and one of them looked at her friend and said, "Remember, before the photographer takes your picture, lick your lips, because moist lips will make you look sensuous."

Now when I was in eighth grade, I could use all the sensuousness I could get. So I went in there, I sat down on the chair to get my picture taken and went, "Oh, yeah, I gotta lick my lips," and I slopped my tongue over my upper lip, right when he took the picture. The yearbook came out and everyone said, "What happened to Miller? He ate his face!"

Everybody has bad days. But it is when you string bad day upon bad day upon bad day that a downward-spiral depression takes place and you can drop to the point where Paul Horne was, to a point where you no longer want to live.

Warning Signs of Depression

This chapter covers warning signs—not of suicide, but of depression, which can and does lead to suicidal behavior. Taken alone, none of these signs is unusual or suspicious behavior for teenagers. Any number of these signs can occur for any number of reasons; certainly, everybody experiences some of them at some point in his or her life. That is why it is necessary to look at the warning signs in their entirety. It is when you begin seeing a pattern of several of them working together that alarm bells should go off.

The warning signs of depression are like the symptoms of a cold. When you have a cold the symptoms are coughing, sneezing, and a runny nose. This is the outward manifestation of what is happening inside the body. You can observe the symptoms, but you cannot see the virus in the bloodstream causing the cold. Similarly, the warning signs of depression are not what is causing the pain. These signs are the outward manifestations of an inward hurt; they are the symptoms of the pain.

Many times teenagers come to me and say, "I hurt because of this particular problem." What they don't understand is that the hurt is not caused by the surface-level problems that are occurring in their lives. These outwardly visible problems are happening because they are hurting. For example, a young man may come to me and say, "I'm really down because I'm getting bad grades." Actually, he is getting bad grades because he is depressed. Kids tend to focus on symptoms instead of dealing with the underlying causes.

All the warning signs we're going to discuss involve a change in the actions or behavior of the depressed person. In order to notice these changes you have to know the person well. Knowing your kids as they grow involves more than just tracking whom they are with and where they are. It also calls for understanding each teenager's normal behavior, being aware when these norms change, and keeping tabs on your children's emotions. Parents, ask yourselves each day, "Do I know how my kids are feeling?"

The warning signs of depression are *subtle* cries for help. Almost always, the family or friends of a suicide or an attempted suicide say they didn't know or suspect that the person was considering killing himself or herself. In actuality they had not recognized the signs, or they had dismissed them. Like a worsening cold, these changes were an indication that the depression was getting steadily more intense.

An overview of the most common warning signs of depression follows. They do not occur in any order, although some indicate a deeper depression than others. In some people you may see one behavior and in others something completely different. This list is meant to offer a wide-ranging perspective that can help you decide whether or not someone is depressed. Remember, it is not one warning sign, but the combination of several, that indicates if and when a parent or friend should be concerned.

1. Sudden change in behavior

The stereotypical image of a depressed person is of one who has gone from being outgoing to being quiet, moody, and withdrawn. This can be true for someone who is usually "up" and sociable. The opposite, however, can also be true. A teen who is normally shy and quiet can suddenly become loud and boisterous because of a need to vent feelings.

A 13-year-old girl I knew who was in junior high had always blended into the woodwork. She was quiet, well-behaved, and unnoticeable. Suddenly she began getting into fights and became very antagonistic toward everyone. Her mother put her in an alternative school for children having problems, and I went to speak at the school. This youngster began crying during the program when I talked about sexual abuse. Afterward I asked a counselor at the school what had happened to cause her to get so upset.

As it turned out, the school had discovered only the day before that this girl had been sexually abused. Her parents were divorced, and she lived with her mother. Her mother, after her car broke down, had found a mechanic who would trade working on her car for spending a night with the 13-year-old. This mother had traded her daughter's sexual innocence for mechanical work. When this happened to the girl, the shock threw her into depression. Since she was normally a quiet person, her reaction was to act out.

Parents who want to be on the lookout for signs of depression must first define their children's basic personalities and behavior patterns. Are they usually shy or outgoing? Do they never get in trouble or are there often problems? Then when a change occurs it will be noticeable. But remember that changes in teenage behavior can also result from drug use or addiction, which is another indication that something is wrong.

2. Dramatic change in appetite
Teenagers' eating habits are unpredictable anyway, so changes in appetite may be hard to recognize. Some people stop eating when they become depressed. They are just not hungry and they pick at their food. Even teenage boys who are normally bottomless pits may lose their appetites when they become severely depressed.

But the opposite is also true. Some individuals eat everything in sight when they feel down. This is often called nervous eating. A weight-conscious young woman may suddenly not care about her weight or figure.

Either overeating or undereating can also indicate that something is physically wrong. The important thing to watch for is an appetite change.

3. Sleeping difficulty
Sleeping difficulty is hard for parents to spot, but it is one of the most common signs of depression among teens. It is difficult to recognize because parents are in their own bed asleep and don't realize that their son or daughter is unable to sleep. The kid tosses and turns all night. If they don't get to sleep until 4:30 a.m., chances are they'll sleep in the next morning. This earns teenagers the lable "lazy" rather than being recognized as a warning sign.

On the other hand, some people try to sleep through their

depression. One young man was so severely depressed that he slept 16 to 18 hours a day. He would wake up, find that he was still emotionally hurting, turn over, and go back to sleep. He was trying to sleep through the problem. But that never works. If the problem is not dealt with, it will be there every time the person wakes up.

I met this same teen in the hospital after a suicide attempt. He had no longer been able to sleep enough to avoid his problems, and he overdosed on pills. Remember that this can go either way: depressed teenagers may either have problems sleeping, or they may be sleeping as much as possible to escape from problems.

4. Poor performance in school

When teenagers are hurting emotionally, it is hard for them to take an interest in what is going on at school. They have an "I don't care" attitude about almost everything. It is difficult to care about who was president in 1864 or how to diagram a sentence when one is in deep emotional pain.

I see this attitude a lot. When teens are depressed, I tell them, "If you get bad grades you're going to flunk."

"I don't care."

"If you flunk, your parents are going to get upset."

"I don't care."

"If they get upset, they'll ground you and you won't be able to go out."

"I don't care."

When kids are physically sick they don't care whether the stock market crashed or they missed an algebra test; emotional pain has the same effect. Students in pain aren't concerned about grade-point averages. Again, they earn the label "lazy" when in fact they are depressed and unable to make the effort. Effort coincides directly with ability to care. If students don't care, they are not going to try. If they don't try, their grades are going to drop.

5. Restless, irritable behavior

Depressed teens are raw bundles of nerves. They are hurting, they are tired of feeling bad, and they get irritable. Approach a depressed teen and casually ask, "How ya doin'," and they're likely to respond, "Just shut up and leave me alone!"

What they are feeling may remind you of cabin fever. You probably remember your last bout: you've spent the whole winter inside, and you have that itchy, anxious feeling. You can't sit still, and you want to change something, but you don't know exactly what. Nothing sounds interesting. You're restless and frustrated. When people make seemingly innocent remarks, you jump all over them. Instead of dealing with the causes of your irritability, it is easier to take it out on the nearest person. Just as with cabin-fever sufferers, some depressed teenagers show all their anger and frustration right on the surface.

6. Unexplained fatigue and that "down" look

This trouble indicator, characterized by a lack of energy and unexplained fatigue, is the opposite of the fifth warning sign. It is best described by the word lethargy. Some depressed kids find it hard to get up the energy or interest to do anything. Their sadness shows physically: their shoulders are slumped and their face is long. How many times have you looked at someone and said, "Is everything all right? You look down."

Kids look sad when they feel sad. I can look at the faces of students in an audience and pick out the ones who are suffering. It shows.

7. Loss of interest in friends

This is a *major* warning sign for adolescents—and for adults as well. Teens are very social beings. They love to be around their own kind, clique, or social group. When kids start pushing friends away it is a clear sign that they are depressed.

Teenagers push friends away for two reasons. First, they can't stand being around people who are happy. When teenagers feel desperately unhappy while everyone else seems to be having a wonderful time, they feel isolated and they hurt even more. Second, depressed teens feel so bad that they may worry about causing pain for others. Not wanting to hurt anyone else, they avoid company, turn down invitations, and withdraw even further into themselves.

Friends call and ask, "Do you want to go to the movies? Do you want to go to the mall? Let's do something together." The depressed teen responds, "No, you guys go without me. I want to stay home tonight."

When a depressed teenager no longer seems to want to be with friends, the friends usually do not recognize this as a warning sign. They too are emotionally immature, and they reject in turn. They perceive being pushed away by their friend as a form of personal rejection: "He doesn't like me any more. Fine, I'll treat him the same way." Hence, friends begin to withdraw, which confirms the depressed person's feelings of being unliked and unlikable.

I use this example with teens: "You're at the lake or the pool in the summer, you look out into the water, and somebody is drowning. How many of you would stroll over to the edge of the water and say, 'Hi. I can swim. Need any help?'

"'Glub, glub, glub.'

"'Sorry to bother you. Have a good one! Hey I tried, but he didn't want my help. There was nothing I could do!'"

That's not what you'd do! If you saw someone drowning you'd kick off your shoes, jerk off your shirt, dive into the water and swim out there to help him.

"Listen," I tell them, "if you are willing to risk your life for a total stranger who is drowning, how much more should you be willing to get involved with your friends who are drowning emotionally? The definition of a true friend is not a person who will stay when times are good. A true friend is a person who will stay even when things go wrong. If someone pushes away, a true friend finds out why."

Paul Horne began pushing his friends away six months before he committed suicide, yet none of them recognized this as a sign of depression. His friends started saying, "What's wrong with Paul? I guess he doesn't like us any more. Well, fine, if he doesn't like us, we don't like him," and they turned their backs on him. I believe that if these teenagers had recognized Paul's behavior as a warning sign, they would have responded more appropriately rather than giving up on him as a friend.

The friendship situation is even more complicated because of the transitions so many families go through—moving, divorces, and job changes. The concept of a true friend is not well developed in this society. Let me say it here: a true friend sticks with you, no matter what.

I have presented *Dare to Live* at one Washington school several years in a row. The last time I spoke there, 16-year-old Pam came up to me after the program. She told me the following story:

Pam's best friend, Amy, had been a good friend since third grade. The two girls lived on opposite sides of town and attended rival high schools, but they had been able to maintain their close friendship through the years.

During the summer following their sophomore year, Amy no longer seemed interested in Pam as a friend. Pam would call her to ask if she wanted to see a movie, go to the mall, or just hang out. Amy turned her down over and over. Finally, Pam got mad, deciding that Amy must have found some other friends and didn't like her any more.

Then one day, Pam was cleaning her room and came across the handout I give kids about the warning signs of depression. She realized that some of these signs, especially the seventh one—loss of interest in friends—seemed to fit the way Amy was acting.

Pam called Amy up immediately. "What are you doing tonight, Amy?"

"Oh, nothing," her friend replied.

"Do you want to do something? We could go to the movies or something."

"No. I don't feel like doing anything," Amy answered.

"Where are your folks?"

"They're out."

Pam persisted. "Where's your brother?"

"He's out on a date," Amy replied.

"If you're home all alone, why don't you come over here?" suggested Pam.

"No, I don't want to. I want to stay home."

"All right, then I'll come over there," Pam persisted.

"No! I don't want you to come over. I've taken a shower, I'm in my pajamas, and I just want to be left alone!"

Pam hung up the phone. Her first reaction was, "Fine, she obviously doesn't want me bothering her," but then she thought about the conversation and decided she couldn't let the matter rest. Pam drove over to see Amy.

Amy answered the door. She reluctantly let Pam in and the two girls began to talk. Within half an hour Amy revealed that she was depressed and feeling very desperate.

About a month later, when Amy was feeling better, she told Pam that she wanted to thank her.

"For what?" asked Pam. "I was just being a friend."

"No, you don't understand," said Amy. "That night you called me and came over, I was going to kill myself. My parents and my brother were gone. I found my dad's gun, and I was going to shoot myself. It was only because you kept bothering me that I didn't do it."

I believe that if teenagers understand this warning sign and have a friend who starts pushing them away, they won't let go. They will reach out to their friend and say, "Hey, you are my friend and I'm sticking by you. You can't push long enough or hard enough to get rid of me. I am your friend."

8. Increased drug and alcohol use

It has been said that the dramatic rise in drug and alcohol abuse is the cause of the mounting teen suicide rate. I disagree. Drug and alcohol abuse does not cause suicide, but it is a way to escape overwhelming feelings of depression. "I will do anything to feel better for just a little while" is the attitude of the abusers.

Our society is inundated with drugs. We turn to drugs for all kinds of problems: when you're sick, when you're sleepy when you shouldn't be or not sleepy when you should be, when you're in pain, when you want to lose weight or gain weight or do better in athletics, and dozens of other reasons. If you can't find it in the drugstore, ask your doctor. If your doctor won't give it to you, then you can ask someone on the street to provide "the cure." You don't have to look far, because in the United States there is a pill or drink that will "solve" any problem.

According to slick television, radio, and magazine ads, you can't have a good time without absorbing chemicals that stimulate your body. The best commercials on television are beer commercials. They are attention-getting, they often use famous faces, and they are aimed at the young. They portray drinking as fun, as a party, as a joke, and as a marvelous time with gorgeous people and clever dogs. Whether you're having a great day, or want to have an even better day, celebrate life with alcohol.

Then there's the opposite message. If you're having a bad day, a drink can make you feel better. According to many television shows, drinking solves all problems: "Had a hard day at the office? Here, let me fix you a martini."

Kids are very television-oriented. They believe the slick messages the media pumps out. This is what teenagers hear and believe: you need to be chemically stimulated in order to feel good and chemically stimulated when you feel bad.

After years of hearing the media message that drinking is good for whatever's ailing you, and observing parents and peers using alcohol and drugs, it is no surprise that hurting kids turn to drugs to deal with pain. The problem is that alcohol and many other drugs are depressants. They mask the pain temporarily, but when the high wears off, the users are plunged deeper into the depression from which they were seeking escape. This roller coaster helps push our young people closer to the edge, closer to suicide.

A young man I met at one school had started smoking dope in seventh grade because his family didn't care about him and smoking made him forget the rejection. Instead of dealing with his problem he chemically induced a short-lived euphoria. But as his hurt increased—because his family never did and never would show that they cared about him—he had to smoke more and more.

The depression he felt because of his poor family life was intensified by his depression from using drugs. He then used more drugs to try to feel better. This kid hurt, and his escape from the pain was drugs. But the crutch he picked created a hell in itself. He eventually took a drug that did the ultimate job of relieving his pain. His death certificate read "accidental death by overdose," but I know that this teen had reached a point at which he began to wonder if life was worth living. He could see no reason to live, so he bailed out.

The message we must give young people is this: *There is no way to get drunk enough or stoned enough to drive a problem away. Every time you come back to reality the problem is still there. The only way to deal with problems is to face them sober and head-on.*

Alcohol and drug abuse not only deepen depression, but they lead to situations that most kids would not have to face if they were to stay away from chemical influences in the first place. No town in the United States has been spared the tragedy of young people dying in car accidents as a result of drinking or drug use. In every city we read headlines about thefts, robberies, and muggings that are sparked by addicts' need for money for drugs.

Even those who are not involved in the drug-and-alcohol scene can get caught up in the excitement of a party and the fun of feeling slightly woozy. Often, however, they too find themselves in situations they can't handle. One young woman told me a story about a Halloween party that changed her life.

Fifteen-year-old Michelle had been invited by her boyfriend to attend a costume party. Her mom gave her permission after being assured that the party would be chaperoned. But when Michelle arrived, she found that there was no adult supervision and all the teens were drinking.

Michelle had never before been drunk. She didn't want to be different, so she accepted a beer. Her boyfriend thought it would be amusing to get Michelle sloshed, so he began adding whiskey to her beer until she was so drunk that she could only sit on the couch and feel sick. Her boyfriend wanted to make out, but Michelle didn't want to. He left her, still drunk, to fend for herself.

While she was in this alcohol-induced fog, another young man found her and took her to a bedroom. With no control over herself because of the alcohol, she found herself having sex with three boys consecutively. Michelle had never had sex before this happened. She later told me that she had felt like two different persons. She knew what was happening was wrong, but she was unable to do anything to stop it. It was only when she began vomiting that the boys stopped assaulting her.

The young men then dressed her, took her home and deposited her on her front step. Michelle was so drunk that the next morning she did not remember telling her mother about the night's events. When she returned to school, she found that the boys who had used her were spreading rumors around school about how easy she was.

After I told this story to another group of high schoolers,

one young woman wrote to me and said that she had been planning to kill herself until she heard Michelle's story. The same thing had happened to her under similar circumstances, and she was contemplating suicide because the aftermath of this terrible incident did not end with her hangover. She learned that boys only asked her out because they'd heard that she would sleep with anyone. This young woman no longer felt that her life was of any value. When she heard about Michelle, however, she decided not to kill herself. "If she can make it through that, so can I," she wrote.

Drugs and alcohol cause depression or worsen a depression that has already begun. Drug and alcohol use, even in a one-time or first-time situation, leads to hurts that teenagers would not have to suffer if they avoided drugs entirely. Teenagers should leave these lethal chemicals absolutely alone.

9. Constant feelings of worthlessness and self-hatred

When you feel good, there's a spring in your step and you see what is right with the world. When in a good mood, I like what I see when I look in the bathroom mirror. But when I'm feeling bad about myself, I can go to the same bathroom, look in the same mirror at the same face, and say "Blecch."

The first thing I see is my nose. It's been broken four times. I've got one ugly shnoz. Then I see the reason why my nose has been broken four times, namely, I'm blind in my right eye. When I was a kid it was crossed. I used to look at my nose all the time.

Kids would tease me, "You know you got a funny-looking eye?"

I'd snap back, "You know you got a funny-looking face?" Then they'd punch me in the nose and break it again.

Then I look at my hair. I used to comb my hair back, but then my forehead started to grow. I wasn't getting any smarter, so I started combing my hair down and my scalp began peeking through behind. So now I'm combing it back again. My grandfather's bald, my dad's bald and both my older brothers are bald. I don't have a whole lot to look forward to.

Then, when I'm really feeling bad, I look at the thing that bothers me the most. That's my overbite. I was in a car wreck a couple years ago, and I damaged the joint of my jaw. I went to an oral surgeon, and as he was looking at it, I said something about my overbite.

He said, "Well, technically, Mike, you don't have an overbite."

"Yeah, sure; what do you call this?" I asked.

"That's an underchin."

"Oh gee, I feel a lot better now. What do you mean, an underchin?"

"Well, look at it like this. When you were developing, you got a size 10 skull and only a size eight jaw. What we're dealing with here is a Major Skeletal Deformity." Now if that doesn't make you feel uglier than homemade sin, nothing will.

Just like my seeing the worst in the mirror when I'm feeling bad, people who are hurting often have "I hate" attitudes. They are very critical of themselves. They look for, and accent, the negative. You hear them say things like "I hate my hair" or "I hate my clothes" or "I hate myself." When people are hurting, nothing satisfies them.

Paul Horne thought he was ugly. In his "Who Am I?" essay, turned in just before he ran away, he wrote, "I sometimes feel that I'm the ugliest person in the world, that I'm a nobody." But no one who sees the picture of Paul Horne taken shortly before his death would say that he was ugly. Self-hatred was yet another sign that Paul was depressed.

When you hear someone say "I hate . . . I hate . . . ," what they are saying is "I hurt . . . I hurt." Depressed people hate themselves because of the emotional pain they are suffering.

10. Excessive risk-taking

Teens are risk-takers. They feel young and invincible. Death seems a long, long way away, as if it only happens to old people. But reckless young people can push life to and beyond its limits, especially when they are feeling bad, angry, or frustrated.

Many times people take out their frustrations and anger behind the wheel of their car. Young men are especially prone to this; when they're going through emotional stress, they respond by driving fast and recklessly.

A lot of suicidal deaths are falsely attributed to accidents. When people are hurting, they don't care what happens to them. Besides, if they are in pain, is being careless really a risk? In addition, they experience an adrenalin surge from anger and fear that temporarily makes them feel better. The resulting "accidents" are directly caused by the pain.

In Washington a young man's girlfriend broke up with him. He piled four friends into his car and took off. He drove like a madman, that is, a hurt and angry young man, until he rolled off an embankment into a river. None of the teenagers died from injuries caused by the accident. All five drowned.

There is a popular saying: "Friends don't let friends drive drunk." We need to teach our children an additional saying: "Friends don't let friends drive mad."

Young women might take other kinds of risks. They might put themselves in situations in which they could be harmed. I know one young woman who would go into a large city and walk through a bad section of it alone, late at night, because she didn't care what happened to her. Another risk might be taking drugs or drinking a little more than usual. Still another might be dating someone who is "dangerous" or who has a bad reputation. Girls do take risks, although predominantly it is young men who take risks with how they drive.

Any kind of risky behavior can temporarily mask depression. The scary part is that the end result of these risks can be permanent and deadly.

11. Preoccupation with death and dying

The Bible says, "Out of the abundance of the heart, the mouth speaks." This means that what is felt inside is mirrored outside. When people are preoccupied with talking about death, dying, or suicide, they are speaking what they feel in their hearts.

In our society we do not talk about death. It would certainly put a damper on a dinner party if, in a conversational lull, someone said, "Well, so which of us is going to die first?" The topic would make everyone uncomfortable and probably kill a few appetites. Instead, we mask death with euphemisms. People speak of "passing away," "departing," or "going to meet their Maker." We don't like to talk about it.

Therefore, when someone is talking about death and dying, it is because they are thinking about it seriously. Paul Horne began talking about suicide six months before he took his life.

Talking is not the only way depressed people express a preoccupation with dying. A young person who is creative may express these feelings by writing a poem about death or by drawing pictures of a graveyard or other symbols of death.

12. Giving away personal or prized possessions

The first teenager I knew who had attempted suicide was a young girl in the bed next to a friend I was visiting in the hospital. This teen had serious problems at home. Her stepfather was sexually abusing her and her mother chose not believe it. This was in 1980, five years before *Dare to Live* was launched, but I was successful in getting help for this girl to protect her in her home. She gradually recovered from her suicide attempt.

One of the last things the young woman had done before she tried to kill herself was to give away everything she owned. She gave away her clothes and her stuffed animals. She gave away her jewelry and her posters. She gave away everything, because she wanted to be remembered.

I tell my teen audiences that if friends call them up in the middle of the night and say, "Hey, I want to give you my stereo," the proper response is not "Gee, thanks! Can I have your records too?" The proper response is to ask questions like, "Why are you giving me this?" If the friend gives a lame excuse such as "I don't need them anymore" or "I want you to have it" or "You'll get more use out of it," it is a clear sign that this person is planning his or her death.

No Warning Signs

A small percentage of teens do not show any warning signs in spite of deep depression. Jennifer, the young woman who committed suicide on the first day of school, gave no outward indications to her friends or family that she was depressed. Friends saw Jennifer the day before she died. They talked to her, and they felt she acted normally. She told one friend how excited she was about beginning her senior year. Jennifer didn't share her pain with anyone. But on the inside she was hurting. Achievers like Jennifer have learned to mask their feelings; these kids do not want to let anyone down.

At another school a cheerleader, Kim, came up after the assembly and very cheerily asked if she could talk to me. I fully expected her to say, "I've got a friend who needs help . . . ," but when we met in the counseling office with the door shut, Kim burst into tears. The mask came off and Kim revealed that she was contemplating suicide. She was overwhelmed and didn't want to live any longer. Kim, too, kept all her pain inside.

Three Stages Toward Suicide

I have found that people go through three stages when considering suicide. First, they think about the act: "I'm going to kill myself. I don't want to live any longer." It was obvious from what Kim said that she was thinking seriously about suicide.

Second, they plan the act: "How am I going to do it? I can shoot myself, overdose, or slit my wrists." I asked Kim if she knew how she would commit suicide. She quickly replied that she was going to take an overdose of pills.

Third, when suicide is imminent, they bring together the implements to do the deed. Kim revealed that she not only had thought through how she would die, but she also had a bottle of pills in her purse that she would use.

This 17-year-old woman had planned her suicide for the next Saturday. She had responsibilities to take care of first. Friday night was the last basketball game of the season, and she had to finish her cheerleading duties so she wouldn't let down the squad. The morning after the game, she planned to die with her responsibilities fulfilled.

It is important to remember that everyone displays these signs at some point, and all of us are depressed at times in our lives. Certainly, all depressed people do not commit or even attempt suicide. But when teenagers are depressed they need attention and support from their friends and family. The problems don't go away if teens ignore them, and the problems don't go away if their parents ignore them either.

The most important thing to look for is a pattern of several of these signs. The more warnings there are, the more concerned a parent or a friend should be.

If young people show warning signs, don't be afraid to talk to them. Ask "What's going on? I noticed this . . ." or "I see a change in you." Just as in the example of the drowning person, you are not going to cause more problems by reaching out. If you don't feel comfortable reaching out, find someone else who can. Don't walk away without trying to help.

Questions and Answers

1. How does one teach kids to deal with bad days?
First, kids have to realize that they *will* have bad days, because bad days happen to everybody. Next, give them an endpoint. Ask them to hang on for 72 hours, and then see how they feel after that. Chances are, circumstances will have turned around. This experience gives kids the knowledge that there is an end to even the worst day. There is always hope that tomorrow, or the next day, or the day after that, will be better.

2. How many warning signs should someone show before I get worried?
I get worried at three or four, but each teenager is different. If a teen is experiencing two or three, then they're probably depressed and you should start looking into the reasons for their depression (see question 9.) If the teen is demonstrating three or four signs, they are pretty well into depression and you should deal with it immediately. Remember, these are warning signs of depression, not of suicide.

3. Are there other reasons teens may show the warning signs?
Again, each individual warning sign may point to many changes taking place during the teen years other than a drop into depression.

Drug and alcohol abuse is one reason kids might exhibit some of these behaviors, as well as being a warning sign itself. But even if a teen isn't depressed to begin with, if he or she is using drugs as something to do or because it's cool, the drug abuse will cause depression and trigger other warning signs.

Another reason kids might demonstrate some of the warning signs has to do with growing up. They might need more "space" and want to spend time in their room alone. That doesn't necessarily mean that they are cutting themselves off from friends and family. Other factors can also cause the warning signs, such as illness or prescription drugs. What you must look for are changes in behavior—changes that persist.

4. How do I know whether my child is eating too much or too little?
Know your child. Look for weight loss; anorexia and bulimia are two fairly common psychological problems that teenage girls and boys face, and these eating disorders have been linked to suicide. If teens continually focus on their weight, even when they are very thin, or if they do a lot of ritualized eating and exercising, you should be concerned. Conversely, if there is a rapid weight gain, if they no longer care how they look or what they eat, you should take note.

You have to know your children and know what is normal for them. Everybody goes on diets. Everybody eats too much at Christmas and Thanksgiving. In the spring it is a rare teenage girl who doesn't go on a diet to get into her bathing suit. Likewise I don't know many guys who don't work out to give themselves a little better physique. Know your children so you can be aware of when they aren't on a normal track.

5. How do I know if my children are sleeping well?
Ask them. I think that every morning parents should ask their kids how they slept. When they were babies you were attuned to that, but when kids get older you probably just *expect* them to go to bed and sleep. Instead, make this a routine question. Keep track of your kids sleeping habits.

6. What does it mean if my kid suddenly has a bunch of new friends?
If your child starts pushing off old friends, this could point to the seventh warning sign, loss of interest in friends. If he or she has picked up new friends, you need to determine who those new friends are. If the new friends use drugs, they may be

the people from whom your child is getting drugs. I'd be very concerned if something like this happened to my child.

7. How can I tell if my child uses drugs and alcohol at all, or if they already do, whether or not they have increased their drug and alcohol use?

It is extremely important that you know the answers to these questions. Sit down and talk to your kids about alcohol and drugs, and about depression. Don't preach or lecture, but explain that drugs and alcohol will worsen a depression. Tell your kids that the worst thing they can do if they are feeling down is to take drugs. Explain that if they take drugs when they're depressed, the drugs will make them hurt more. Kids need to know that.

Also watch for the other warning signs, especially for drops in grades or attitude problems. Look also at the physical signs listed in the chapter on drug and alcohol abuse. You must pay very close attention: drug and alcohol abuse is not an easy thing to determine.

8. Can kids get depressed and not give out any warning signs?

About 10 percent don't reveal any warning signs at all; they keep everything inside. These are often kids who follow the straight and narrow, have everything together, and give no reason for their parents to worry. They get good grades and seem socially happy. But these teenagers may hurt, too.

Even if your child causes no problem at all, you still need to say to them, "I know you hurt sometimes. No one goes through life with everything perfect and nothing wrong." Let them know that you understand that they hurt. That understanding breaks down the wall so they can open up and talk to you.

9. If my child is showing these warning signs, where do I go for help?

First, talk to the child. Next, talk to the school, your minister, or a counselor. Try to find out the reason for the teenager's depression. What is causing them to feel this way? What is going on in their life? Your kid might look at you and say, "I don't know what's wrong," or they'll deny that they feel bad. In that case other sources, including your child's friends, can help you figure out what is happening.

Everybody gets depressed, so everybody will give out warning signs at one time or another. What you must try to combat is the depression, not the warning signs. If your child can't eat, can't sleep, and is getting poor grades in school, don't decide merely to get a tutor, to play relaxing music at night, and to make their favorite meals. Those "solutions" deal with the symptoms; they do not address the underlying problem.

If your teenager is not willing to share with you the reason for their depression, remember Rob's story in Chapter One. He didn't want to tell his parents how he felt because what he had done was against everything his parents had taught him and believed in. If your child will not open up to you, for whatever reason, you must find someone whom the teen will trust.

Finally, realize that the reasons behind depression are often situations for which you won't have an answer. Often there is nothing that can be done except to help your child walk through the hurt they are experiencing.

4

How to Help

"Whoever preserves one life, it is as if he preserved an entire world."

— Talmud

In my six years as chaplain with the fire department, I spoke to at least 500 teenagers in the hospital following suicide attempts. With one voice, all of them said they hadn't opened up before their attempts because they had no *one* to talk to. This is not true. The problem for these teens was not that there was no one to talk to, but that they did not know *how* to communicate their pain.

"No one understands" was the common theme I heard from these teens. Why did they think that nobody would understand? Communication fails at such a crucial time for many reasons. Some teens feel isolated and confused; they think that no one else in the world feels as bad as they do, that there is no one who can relate to their problems. Other teens have not been taught to expect any pain in life or how to communicate these feelings when they occur. Still other teens "shut down" when their attempts to talk to someone have been unsuccessful. Let's look at each of the reasons that teens may keep their problems inside until they are so desperate that death seems the only solution.

Teens Relate to Parents Who Aren't "Perfect"

There is a thinking process in adolescence that goes like this: "I don't understand what is going on inside of me. If I don't understand it, then no one else will either."

While I do not blame parents, I have observed that many adults unconsciously encourage the teen's mistaken belief that "no one understands" by not admitting that parents make mistakes. Rare are the parents who seek forgiveness for their mistakes. Few even share with their children the feelings and frustrations of the days when they, too, were teenagers. All parents were once teenagers who became depressed, had bad times, and were eventually able to overcome their problems. Adolescents need to hear this specific information from adults.

The idea that "my parents are perfect; they can't relate to my problems" develops gradually during the long-term relationship between parent and child. When children are young, parents tell them when to get up and what to wear. They buy their clothes, tell them what to eat, and generally foster an image of the perfect parent who knows everything and never makes mistakes.

Consequently, kids grow up with the idea that their folks are never wrong and never troubled. When teens feel bad or face problems, they conclude: "Mom and dad won't understand because they haven't gone through this."

Parents have experienced virtually everything their kids are experiencing, and they must tell that to their kids. As you teach children to eat vegetables and put on warm clothes when it is cold outside, you must also teach them about the issues and problems they will face as they grow into adults. They must learn that fear, anger, and suffering are not unique to teenagers; that from childhood to adolescence to maturity to old age everyone experiences the whole spectrum of life's highs and lows. We can't expect our children to comprehend these lessons automatically.

Kids love to hear stories about when their parents were young. This is an ideal way to relate the scary, sad, upsetting, exciting, and wonderful experiences that parents have had — and are still having as adults — to the experiences that their kids are now having.

Share All Aspects of Life

Don't be uneven in what you teach your children. Parents and kids need to discuss physical, mental, emotional, and spiritual experiences. Each of these four aspects is of equal importance because the teenager will have experiences and problems in all four areas. Neglect in one or more areas stunts a young person's growth.

Let's look at some examples: If you teach your children spiritually, mentally, and emotionally, but neglect the physical aspect of their lives, they are likely to have poor physical hygiene and problems with their teeth, and they may become ill because of neglect. If you teach your children physically, emotionally, and spiritually, but not mentally, they'll grow up not knowing how to read, write, or do simple arithmetic. If you take care of children physically, mentally, and spiritually, but don't give them emotional insight, you will leave them vulnerable to all the different emotional upheavals in their lives. The same goes for spiritual growth. If you don't teach spirituality, your child may grow up without the basic moral fiber needed to be successful and happy in our society. (For more details, see Chapter Nine, "Balance and Self-Esteem.")

With teenagers who attempt suicide, the aspect of growth that has been most often neglected is the emotional one. Suicidal kids usually don't understand either that they are depressed or why. Parents can remedy that. Teens should be taught that they will have broken hearts. They will have friends who treat them without respect, and some people will let them down. They will experience the joy of winning and suffer the pain of losing something important to them. These are common emotional experiences that kids should be told to expect.

Be There to Listen

Not only must young people be taught that they will have problems, but parents must be there to listen and to understand when the problems arise. Everyone wants to be understood. There is nothing worse for a teenager than trying to confide in someone and having that person respond with a look that says, "I don't have the foggiest notion of what you're talking about." If you, as parents, want your kids to come to you when they're happy *and* come to you when they're sad, then they must trust that you understand them. Only when they know you understand will they communicate at all times. There is nothing more crucial to your role as parent of a teenager than to listen and understand. *The ability of parents to understand the intensity of teenagers' emotions and to support them during rough times is probably the most important factor in the prevention of teen suicide.*

When a hurting teen reaches out, how can parents best offer their support? Parents need to express *empathy*, the appreciative sharing of another's emotions or feelings. Many people confuse empathy with sympathy. There are differences. *Sympathy* is entering into someone else's mental state in such a way that there is an emotional involvement. In other words, sympathy involves experiencing the other person's emotions and leads to feelings of pity or compassion. Parents who respond with sympathy, however, may become too emotionally involved to offer a child much support. Parents who respond with empathy, on the other hand, can understand the emotions of teenagers without feeling overwhelming sorrow or pity for them.

When a 15-year-old breaks up with his or her first girlfriend or boyfriend, or when a teen really likes someone but those feelings aren't returned, he or she is in pain. Parents can let teenagers know they understand by being empathetic: "It does hurt. You will get over it, although that is hard to believe now. It happened to me and I recovered, even though it was tough. I'm glad that I got through it, because eventually I met someone else." This doesn't deny the adolescent's feelings, and it gives a positive message: Life does go on. Now the teen does not suffer alone, but instead knows that "other people have experienced what I am going through and they are happy now. I will be happy again."

Of course, before parents and teenagers can forge a common bond of understanding, they must be able to communicate. *It is the parents' responsibility to teach communication to their children. It is also the parents' responsibility to initiate communication, because the child is the learner and the parent is the teacher.* Don't sit and wait for your child to come to you. Go to them and talk to them.

When adolescents are depressed, they need, above all else, to talk about what is troubling them. Although there are literally hundreds of people to whom they may talk, not everyone at any given time will talk to them. Put another way, *all* their friends, family, and acquaintances will talk to them at some point in time, but not all will talk to them at *the* time and on *the* subject they need to discuss. Out of those hundreds who will talk, some will not listen. This doesn't mean the teen's problem is unimportant. It does mean that they need to find the right person — one who is willing to listen.

Again, teens interpret anyone's unwillingness to talk to them as confirmation that "no one understands what I'm going through." Then they close up. When a teen is depressed, discouraged, or just lonely, they must decide they will look, and keep looking, until they find the person willing to listen, to talk, and to help them with their problem.

As a door-to-door vacuum cleaner salesman in college, I was told the following by a very wise man: "You will get 10 doors slammed in your face before one person speaks to you. Then, out of every 10 people who will listen to your pitch, only one will let you in their house to show the vacuum cleaner." Not only was he right, but of the people who let me into their houses, it took three tries before one would buy the product. That meant I had to knock on 300 doors and get 299 rejections before someone would listen to my spiel, let me do a demonstration, and then buy a vacuum cleaner.

The man who taught me this rule also gave me a positive way of looking at all that rejection. "Every time a door is slammed in your face," he said, "you are one person closer to making a sale." I knew, because I was told, that I could expect rejection as a door-to-door salesman. Teens need to be told that they may also face rejection when looking for someone who will listen to their problems; they need to consider this search for the right listener in light of the door-to-door salesman. Every time a depressed teen reaches out, but is unable to connect with one of the 200 or so friends, family members, or community people that they know, they are that much closer to finding someone who will listen to them. *They must keep looking to find that person, because that person is out there waiting to be found.*

WHERE TO FIND HELP:
A resource list for parents and teens

1. Family
Each individual is related to a huge network of people by blood or marriage. The wonderful thing about most families is that they are accepting. They have known and loved the teenager since he or she was small. I tell teens to talk to their immediate family — mother, father, sisters, and brothers — or

to their extended family, especially aunts, uncles, cousins, or grandparents. Stepparents, stepsiblings, and godparents also make the list of family resources.

Families are often an ideal outlet for a troubled person, but it doesn't always happen that way. At one middle school a seventh-grade girl, Lisa, came to me after an assembly and told me she was being abused at home. She was lucky enough to have a fine counselor at her school who sat down with this young girl and talked to her. Then he called Lisa's mother. Her mother said, "She's a liar. Tell her not to come home."

In my experience 75 percent of the children who are being molested at home by their father or stepfather and who report the situation to their mother are not believed. (Mothers also sexually abuse children, but statistically this is a much rarer, or less reported, event.) The counselor asked Lisa who in her family loved her, and she told him that she had a grandfather in Denver. When the counselor called her grandfather he made plans to be on the next plane.

Unfortunately, when parents don't believe what their children report, the kids often give up on communicating their problem to anyone else. They could go outside the family and talk to teachers, parents of their friends, clergy, and others. But instead, deciding that nobody cares, they refuse to talk to anyone.

2. Friends

I encourage teens to go to their friends to talk, but friends should be wise enough to know when the problem is more difficult than they can handle. They must be able to say, "Hey, I'm only 15. I don't know what to do about this."

Kids come to me with problems that I, an experienced counselor, can't handle. I'm not ashamed to say I don't know what to do, but I can and will find out. It is shameful to know about the problem and choose not to do anything.

Teens have friends in a multitude of places: at school, in their neighborhood, in their church or temple, on teams, in clubs or organizations, and at work. Friends are often easier for a troubled teen to approach than are adults. It is natural for kids to share problems with each other, since they feel a peer can relate to them. But if teens share their problems with a friend and that friend is not helpful, they should never stop trying to find someone who will help.

Many schools have peer support groups. Sometimes they are called "natural helpers" or "peer counselors." These are fellow students specially chosen and trained to listen. These kids know when to go for additional help and where to find it. They are an excellent resource for a teenager who is not ready to talk to an adult.

I also encourage students to avail themselves of friends' parents. At one school I did a student program during the day and a parent program in the evening. Many of the students came back to hear me speak a second time. One girl told me afterward about a problem she was working through. Her father had died two months before, her mother was grieving, and she was unable to talk to her mother about her feelings.

The mother of another student overheard our conversation, came up to the girl and said, "Honey, I know what you're going through, and I know what your mom's going through. If you need someone to talk to, here is my phone number. Your mom can't talk to you now, so I'll be there for you."

3. School

At school there are teachers, counselors, administrators, coaches, drug and alcohol counselors, and support staff who like kids and care about what happens to them. If they don't know how to help the student, they will refer them to a resource that can help.

People forget that when a suicide or suicide attempt occurs at a school, it is not just the students who are devastated. Everyone who knew the teen feels some responsibility. Teachers and staff are no exception. Stacie, whose suicide was discussed in Chapter One, had a teacher who talked to her mother because he was worried that something he had done had driven Stacie over the edge. Schools are very involved with the young people they teach, and when kids attempt and commit suicide, the teachers and administrators feel part of the blame.

At every school there is a teacher to whom students relate especially well. A perfect example is Ellen Boggs, a health and physical education teacher at Fort Vancouver High School in Vancouver, Washington. Ellen was the teacher who received Paul Horne's "Who Am I?" essay the day he ran away. Since Paul's death, she has asked me to visit her class each semester to talk about depression and suicide.

Teachers such as Ellen have dedicated their lives to education; the vast majority of them let kids know that they like what they are doing and truly care about the students they have chosen to teach. I have the utmost respect for teachers. They have one of the hardest jobs in our society today. If an individual cares enough to be a teacher and to be dedicated to working with young people, they are usually a good person for a depressed teen to approach.

4. Community Resources

There are many people in every community who are devoted to helping those in trouble. Police officers, firefighters, and religious leaders have chosen to work in these fields because they want to help. Students also should not overlook the availability of many community workers and volunteers who are concerned about what happens to young people.

When I first became a youth minister at age 21, there wasn't anyone working with the teenagers at our church. Starting with a couple of kids from the neighborhood, I let it be known that I cared about teenagers and would be there for them. We commenced with a Monday-night Bible study with two or three teens. By the end of the school year more than 80 kids jammed into our house on Monday evenings. I spent seven years as a youth minister, and during that time I talked to literally thousands of kids. In virtually all communities there are religious organizations that focus on youth and are willing to help young people with problems. If you, as a parent, are reading this book and want to know how you can help, this is where you can fit in. You don't have to be a psychologist, counselor, or youth minister to help kids. If your home is open, warm, and loving, they will come to you, and you can provide the service of being there and listening. Start by being available and letting kids know you care.

5. Emergency Programs
Every community has programs aimed at emergency situations. There are teenage talk lines, suicide-prevention hot lines, counseling services, chaplains with police and fire departments, YMCA, YWCA, and drug- and alcohol-abuse programs.

You can call the emergency room at a hospital and explain the situation, and they can direct you to an agency that will help. If it is two a.m. and there seems to be no one available, call 911 or the local police or fire dispatch number. Emergency response teams would much rather have a chance to help *before* a suicide attempt than deal with the end result.

6. Professional counselors, psychologists, and psychiatrists
Referrals to professional help for a depressed student are often made through the school or at the parents' request. There is a wide variety of mental-health-care professionals who work with people of all ages to resolve depression. It doesn't matter who you call as long as you do call.

In indirect ways, Paul Horne tried to communicate to his friends and family that he was depressed. Friends heard him saying, "I wish I were dead," and his "Who Am I?" essay was a cry for help. Too often the cry from young people like Paul is indirect. They want someone to come to them; they want someone to rescue them from themselves. These teens have reached the point where they believe, "If someone really cared for me or understood me, they would pick up my signals and know that I am hurting."

As depression deepens, there is a point when a person will no longer reach out or becomes unable to reach out for help. That's when others have to see what is happening. Read the signs and seek help for that individual. Reach out to them.

A number of kids who attempted suicide told me something like this: "I did it so people would know how much I hurt. They'd know I needed help." My response was, "If you'd died, it wouldn't matter what people thought because you wouldn't have been here." In these kids' minds their suicide attempt was another cry for help. It's as if it never dawns on depressed teenagers that once they've died, they're dead — permanently.

Don't wait for a crisis. Find out what support is available for your teens before they need it. Talk to them about the options. Tell them, "If you are hurting and you don't feel like you can come to me or I'm part of the problem, here are people you can reach out to." Just as you give them a number to call if their car breaks down, help your kids come up with six to eight names and phone numbers of groups and individuals who will be there when they need them. Refer to the "support" sheet in the back of this book for ideas.

According to various of studies, between 35 and 90 percent of young people seriously consider suicide at some time during their adolescent years. All teens should have this information on hand now. It is best to arm kids with contact information in advance, so they will know where to turn for themselves or a friend if they get into a situation that feels desperate. To help teens compile a resource list also tells them that you understand that depression happens, that you will support them, and that you care about what happens to them.

Gresham Union High School

I was working at the fire department at the time I was taking that prescription for Corgard, and the chief asked me to run an errand for him. I loved running errands for the chief, because I loved driving his car.

I got on the freeway fully expecting to have a good time in the chief's car, but driving down 78th Street, I saw a dead cat on the side of the road.

Now let me say something here, seriously. If I say anything to offend anyone today I apologize, because I'm not here to offend you. I'm here because I care. But in all honesty, I don't like cats. When I see a dead cat I think the world is a little better place to live. I know there are some cat lovers out there who will disagree with me.

But this particular day I see this dead cat, and I'm so depressed and hurting so bad, honestly, I start to cry. "Poor little kitty, kitty." Sniff, sniff.

In my mind's eye I see this little eight-year-old girl standing at the door of her house, calling, "Here puddy tat. Here kitty."

This old flat cat ain't never coming home. You're going to have to get a shovel to get him off the side of the road. It was the saddest thing I ever saw. I cried all the way to Portland. I cried all the way back to Vancouver. I cried two hours over this dead cat!

I get back to the fire station and I'm scrubbing at my face. "O.K., Mike, get a hold of yourself," and I walk in.

Donna, the secretary, says, "Mike, what is wrong with you?"

"What do you mean?"

"Your eyes, they are all red and swollen and puffy . . . hay fever!" She'd think I'd lost my mind if I told her I'd cried over a flat cat. She gave me some Allerest.

I was taking a class at the time and had to write a term paper — footnotes, the whole nine yards. I wrote this term paper and it had to be typed, and I don't know how to type. So I called Jodie, a friend of mine, and said, "Jodie, would you type this report for me?"

Jodie asked, "How long is it?"

"Thirty pages."

"Ohhh nooo."

"Please, Jodie, I'll pay you. I need this typed."

She said, "You don't have to pay me. You're my friend. I'll type it for free."

That day she called me at the fire station and said, "Mike, your report's done. Come by the house and pick it up after work."

So after work I drove over. Jodie is very conscientious about things being done correctly, so as she handed me the report she asked, "How is it?"

I read the first page and was halfway through the second page when I saw that she'd changed something. I asked, "Jodie, why did you change this?"

And honestly, this is all she said: "Mike, your sentence structure was not correct, and I changed it so the paragraph would flow better."

Have you ever had somebody say one thing to you and you heard something else? What I heard Jodie say was this: "Mike, you're a moron. You write like a chimpanzee. If I had typed what you had written, people would think I was as ignorant as you are!"

Oooh, it made me mad that she changed my report! I glared at her, and I said, "Jodie, if you can't do what I ask you to do, don't bother doing it at all!" and I ripped the report in half.

Honestly, I know you won't believe this, but she got mad. (Jodie is my friend and full-time associate at Dare to Live. This is a true story. You can ask her. I had to crawl on my hands and knees to get forgiveness for what I did.)

Guys, I want to tell you something. This has nothing to do with the assembly. This is a freebie. If you're ever out with a young lady and she starts to yell at you, don't worry about it, because girls just naturally like to yell.

Any of you girls disagree with that? I can prove it. How many of you girls have a younger brother, and how many of you guys have an older sister, and all the guy ever hears is this: "Get out of my *room! I'm going to tell mom!"*

True? If a girl is yelling at you, don't worry about it, O.K.? It is when they start to whisper that you'd better take notice.

Jodie looked daggers at me and whispered, "Don't you ever, ever ask me to do anything for you again as long as you live." I couldn't believe it! She was mad at me!

I scowled at her and said, "Don't worry, I won't," and I threw the report at her. Up it went, down it came.

Jodie clamped her jaw tight, and a muscle in her jaw started to bulge. When that muscle starts to bulge, Jodie is going to do one of two things. One, she's going to slap the snot out of you. Two, she's going to throw something very heavy and hard at your head. Either way I knew it wasn't a very safe place to be. So I left.

I'm driving home and thinking, "Mike, what a terrible thing to do. What an awful way to treat your friend. Come on, snap out of this!" Besides, I didn't have a report to turn in. I wasn't going to go back and say, "Uh, do you think I could have the rough draft back, please?"

Well, things went on like that for a long time, and I didn't snap out of it. My poor wife thought I was losing my mind. First thing I'd do when I got home was take the phone off the hook. I'd say, "Don't put the phone back on the hook. I don't want to talk to anybody. I don't want to see anybody." If someone came over to the house while I was there, I'd go hide in the back room until they left. I just wanted to be left alone.

It was while I was sitting in the back room one day that I decided I no longer wanted to live. I decided my wife would be better off without me, my children would be better off without me, and, for that matter, the entire world would be better off without me.

I thought, "How am I going to kill myself?" I decided I would shoot myself, but I didn't have a gun.

So that night I drove over to my brother's house — he's a gun collector — and said, "Larry, I need to borrow a pistol."

He asked, "What for?"

"There's a burglar in our neighborhood," I said. "He's broken into a few houses on our street, and I need a gun to protect my home."

Larry said, "I've got just the gun for you, Mike." He went to his gun cabinet and came back with a .45-caliber Colt automatic. He loaded the clip with hollow-point bullets. He slammed the clip into the butt of the gun and said, "Mike, anybody comes to your house, you point this at them, and you pull the trigger. You hit them, you kill them. If you miss them, they'll die of a heart attack."

I said, "That's what I need, Larry. That's it." I took the gun. I hid it under the front seat of the car; I didn't want my wife or kids to find it. Then I proceeded to go home. That was Thursday night. I decided that Friday I would go to work as usual since it was payday and I knew my wife would need the money. Then on Saturday I would tell my wife I had to work overtime, and I would drive up into the hills and shoot myself.

Friday, I went to work. They gave me my paycheck, and at 5 o'clock I stopped at the bank. Everybody and their dog was at the bank on Friday at 5 o'clock. I'd been going to the same bank for years, and when I walked up to the teller, she said, "Hi, Mike! How ya doin'?"

Now, everybody says that. It's a common greeting. I said reluctantly, "I'm all right. I'm fine." And then I started to cry, just because she asked me how I was doing! I started repeating, "I'm all right," tearing up, sniffling all over the place.

Grace, the teller, looked at me and said, "Mike, what is wrong with you? You act like you have PMS."

Honestly, that's what she said.

I said, "I really don't think so."

"I know that!" Grace said, but she took me by the hand, led me around the teller's cage, and took me back to the employees' lunchroom. "Mike, I know you don't have PMS, but listen. Seriously, I used to cry one week out of every month, and I went to the doctor and he gave me something for it. You need to go to the doctor. This isn't normal."

It was as if a light went on. I was already going to the doctor. I was taking something. I said, "Can I use the phone?"

She said, "Sure," and I called my doctor. He was just leaving for the hospital.

"Listen, you've got to help me," I said. "I need to know, is there any chance, any possibility at all, that Corgard can cause depression?"

I'll never forget what he said. "Sure Mike, big time."

"OOOOhhhhhh. I cried two hours over a flat cat, my friends hate me, my wife thinks I'm losing my mind, and I'm crying in a bank because a teller asked me how I was doing."

He said, "Maybe you ought to stop taking it, Mike." Oh, good deduction, Sherlock. "Mike, listen, I'm leaving for the hospital now but I want to see you tomorrow morning. I'm closed, but I'll come down here at 7 o'clock. I'll open the clinic. I want to see you."

The next morning I drove to the clinic, instead of up in the hills where I'd planned to kill myself at 7 o'clock that morning. I had come within 14 hours of taking my life! I saw the doctor and said, "Tell me, how long will it be until I feel good again?" I'd been depressed for five months.

He said, "Mike, I'm not going to lie to you. You've been on the stuff for a long time. It will probably take four to six weeks to come out of this depression."

Here I'd been depressed for five months, and he's telling me I have to hang on at least another month. But as soon as he told me I was going to get over it, I felt better. There was hope. There was light at the end of the tunnel.

HOW TO HELP SOMEONE WHO IS DEPRESSED OR SUICIDAL

We can tell our kids where to go for help, but what do we do when they come to us? The next section will teach anyone — parents, friends, counselors, others — how to help someone who is suicidal. If we tell teens they have to reach out when they're down, then we have to be there when they reach out to us. I will refer to the depressed person as a teenager, but this information applies to any person who is depressed.

Depression is a normal, natural state that everyone goes through now and then. It begins slowly, and if not dealt with, it gradually deepens. I divide depression into two stages, although it actually progresses as a continuum. The stages correspond to how difficult it is to get the depressed person to open up.

Depression's First Stage: Teens Open Up Easily

In the first stage of depression teens are usually willing to talk. If you recognize that a kid is depressed (see the warning signs in Chapter 3), go to them and ask, "What's the problem?" The key to helping in early depression is listening and being direct. Communicate your concern and support. Let them know you care, and that they are important to you. But let them do the talking. You must listen.

If their problem is something totally out of your control — if they are depressed because they have acne or are overweight, if they got grounded after a fight with their parents over grades — there may be little that you as a listener can readily do. However, you can lend an empathetic ear. The teen may tell that he or she us being abused. If you aren't a counselor, that is another type of problem you cannot directly help them with. You can assist by locating professional help.

Just remember that regardless of whether you view a depressed teens' problem as trivial or serious, it is of grave concern to *them*. That's why at this stage of another's depression the most important thing you can do is to become a listening post so that they can talk about what is bothering them and get it out in the open.

How does listening help? When depressed teens keep their problems inside, the problems loom larger and larger until they consume the teens' thoughts and lives. It's like worrying about a problem late at night. You lie in bed and stew over it until it seems insurmountable. But when the sun comes up and you are busy with day-to-day existence, the problem seems smaller, even solvable, because you are able to put it back into perspective. Bringing a problem from the dark recesses of your thoughts and discussing it with another person gives it that same daylight perspective. Once teenagers state the problem clearly, they often feel better because it seems less overwhelming.

Listeners don't have to do anything about the problem. They don't have to come up with the solutions. They don't have to fix what is bothering the depressed person. They only have to listen and care.

Listening Skills

Now, that's not quite as simple as it sounds. Some ways of listening are more helpful than others. Think about the people to whom you like to talk. Chances are that they are not just good talkers but also good listeners. There are techniques to being a good listener. Everyone can benefit by learning a few of these listening skills.

First, find a place where you will be undisturbed, take the phone off the hook, and remove distractions. If a depressed teen needs to talk, don't do something else such as cooking dinner or paying bills. Even if you can do two things at once, the person who is talking will feel that your attention is divided. Also, don't interject your own problems. The hurting person feels better when you pay attention to them.

Physically you must give the speaker your complete regard. Make sure your body language says you are concentrating. Fidgeting and twitching indicate impatience. Sit quietly, maintain eye contact, and stay focused. This lets them know they are special and important.

If you want to show someone that you care, be a good listener. Be willing to put down what you are doing and listen when they need to talk. Treat whatever they are discussing as if it is of the utmost importance. To them it is. Give them your undivided attention.

Depression's Second Stage: Convince Teens You Care

In the second stage of depression teenagers often don't want to talk. Their depression may have deepened to the point that they no longer care. Once they've crossed that line, it becomes doubly hard to get them to open up and tell you what is wrong. They can even become belligerent and hostile. (Remember the fifth warning sign number — agitation.) These teens have been locked into their problems for so long that they don't want to talk about them, because bringing them to the surface hurts. Their attitude is that nobody cares or understands anyway.

The way to reach someone in the second stage of depression depends on the individual. There are many ways of getting through. For me, being loving and gentle sometimes works. Other times I have to argue or browbeat them. The approach depends on the person and their personality. When the depressed person is resisting, do whatever it takes to get them talking.

You can be straightforward: "Don't tell me that you don't have a problem. Everything about you tells me that you do."

You can go through the back door: "I need your help. Your sister is having some problems and I don't know how to deal with them." You are enlisting the depressed teen's help for another purpose, but it tells them that you are willing to listen and you can be trusted. Then you can gently, gradually, turn the conversation around to them.

You can use anger: "I know there's something wrong. You know there's something wrong. But you leave me on the out-side hurting. It makes me mad." This is manipulation, but it is also a way to get a response. Everything is fair when a life may be on the line.

You can tease or joke. If you laugh along with depressed teens, you project a different outlook on life. These kids bottle up their emotions. Release, including laughter, makes emotions rise to the surface and become reachable. Do whatever it takes to get the door open.

What's important is not how the message is conveyed, whether angrily or lovingly, but that young people get the message that you do care and are not going to give up or turn your back on them, that you will continue to reach out to them no matter what. Let them know that you aren't doing this because you are stubborn, but because you are concerned. These kids will only open up when they are convinced that you really care.

At many high schools where I speak, I return three or four days in a row until all the hurting kids have had a chance to talk to me. They are not coming to me because of what I say. What I say at schools and in this book is basic common sense. The reason hundreds of teens pour their hearts out to me, a stranger, is simply that they know I care.

Above all else, you must be persistent. By showing your love you are disproving their feelings that no one cares. They have to believe that no matter how hard they push away, you will not give up on them.

What depressed teenagers experience as they look for help can be likened to consulting a doctor because you have an unusual pain. You don't know what the problem is, but you see a doctor because you're looking for someone who will understand. Few things are more frustrating than not knowing what is wrong and realizing that the doctor doesn't know either. Then the second doctor you visit can't figure it out, and after the third doctor you may give up on the medical profession because "nobody understands." Perhaps you don't know how to express your problem, or the doctor doesn't know what is going on. The end result is the same. You give up.

Depressed adolescents have had the same experience. In the early stages of depression the teen may have tried to explain to someone how they felt. No one understood or listened, so they became more depressed and finally become unwilling to talk. To talk to these kids you have to convince them that you care, understand, and will listen.

THREE STAGES TO SUICIDE PREPARATION

Once you've convinced the adolescent that they have to talk, find out whether they are feeling suicidal, and if so, how far along they are in their desire to commit suicide. There are three stages to suicide preparation. Here are some questions and verbal clues you can use to determine what stage the teen is in, and, subsequently, what steps need to be taken to get help. You must be direct in finding out the details.

Stage One: Thinking about the act

"I don't want to live anymore."

"What do you mean, you don't want to live? Why?"

"Everything is going wrong. I'm ugly. I'm flunking math. I just hate myself."

"What are you going to do about it?"

"I'm going to kill myself."

The next question is, "But how?"

If they are nonspecific — "I don't know. I just want to die. Maybe I'll shoot myself, I don't care" — they have not reached stage two. They are still considering the options.

Stage Two: Planning the act

When asked "How?" the teen may reply, "I'm going to shoot myself." If they make a definite, specific statement and are not considering other options, they are in stage two.

The listener then needs to determine if they've gone into stage three by asking, "Why would you choose that method?"

Again, the specificity of the answer indicates how seriously they are considering following through. "Because it seems quick" tells you that they are in a suicidal mind set, but are still in the planning stages.

Stage Three: Gathering the implements for the deed
"Why would you shoot yourself?"
"Because my dad has a gun and I know where it is."
This answer indicates that suicide is imminent. The teen not only has considered the act and planned it, but has the tools available to complete the suicide. Remember, the more details provided about a planned suicide, the greater the risk of follow-through.

If the depressed teenager is still in stage one, you have time to work out the problems by talking. If they are in stages two or three, you must act quickly.

A few weeks after I spoke at a high school in Washington, I received a letter from the school administrator. One of the students had listened. After I encouraged the students to look for help, this boy had talked to his mother. She brought him to school for help. They discovered that he had not only decided to commit suicide, but had stolen his grandfather's pistol, written a note of explanation to his brother, and composed a will. The only thing stopping him from completing the act was that he wanted to wait until after the Christmas holidays; he didn't want to ruin them for his family. This young man was obviously in stage three. We had to help him immediately, or it would have been too late.

If you believe, sense, or are told by a teen that he or she is feeling self-destructive, trust your suspicions and act on them. Your influence may make the difference between life and death. *Treat all threats of suicide as serious and imminent.*

What To Do if the Person Has
Reached Stage Three

1. Take the means away from them.
Remove the gun, pills, or whatever they are planning to use to kill themselves.

2. Make them promise that they won't hurt themselves until they have talked to you first.
Make the teen come to you before they make a suicide attempt. If they tell me, "I can't promise that," I get mad.

"You've come to me and told me about your problems, and I have this huge responsibility for you, but you won't give me the courtesy of allowing me a chance to help? I'll carry the guilt of knowing I didn't do everything I could for you. You at least owe me a chance to try to help." Make them promise that they'll come to you before they act because you care and you will hurt if they die.

This is another instance in which you must do and say whatever you can to get the teen through this critical time. Depressed teenagers do not think about dying because they want to hurt anyone else, but because they are hurting and dying seems to be the only way to stop the pain.

Explain to them how you feel: "If you do anything, it is going to hurt me. Because we've talked, it is only fair to give me a chance to talk you out of it." Kids believe in doing what is fair.

Make a contract, get a verbal agreement, a promise — whatever — that forces them into stopping and talking to you first. To insist on this lets them know that someone is concerned about them.

3. Encourage them to postpone the decision for as long as possible.

Postponing a decision to commit suicide buys time. Ask for the longest period you can get. Three months is a good place to start, but take three days if that is all they can give you. Depression has an end point. The more time you can get, the more support can be built and the better the chances that they will recover from their depression.

"All I'm asking is to give it three months (three weeks, three days) and let's see if during that period we can work it out. If the problems can't be resolved, at least we've tried. If you kill yourself now, you're going to be dead for a long, long time."

You know that depression will end. Psychologically, buying time also gives them an out. Either way, they are looking at an end point. They will get better, or they won't have to deal with the pain anymore because they will kill themselves. Waiting a predetermined amount of time can also help them come out of depression because the problems no longer seem insurmountable. One way or the other, the problems will be solved. Time heals all wounds. Get the depressed kid to allow the time for healing to begin.

Don't believe they've changed their mind about committing suicide if there seems to be a sudden change of heart. I've worked with students who threatened suicide and then backed away from the threats. But I did not necessarily believe they'd changed their minds. Sometimes depressed teens give themselves a finish time — after the state track meet, after the prom, or after the weekend. They have a sense of calm, knowing that they only have to make it through a limited amount of time.

Even if they are no longer threatening suicide, help has to be found for the problems that caused the depression in the first place. A threat of suicide should be taken, and treated, as seriously as a suicide attempt.

4. Don't minimize their problems.

When young people come to you with problems, do not say "Is that all?" and give them a list of others whose problems are bigger. With good reason they'll get mad at you. They are legitimately hurting. You can't tell them they have no right to hurt; everyone has that right. If you go to the doctor because you have a sprained back, you don't need the doctor to say, "You only have a sprained back? I deal with people with heart problems and cancer all the time. This is nothing."

A lot of parents minimize: "You think that's bad, wait until you're an adult." The pressures that adults face are greater than those of most teens, but to kids, the pressures they face are major, and they are happening *now*. Kids' emotions are as real and legitimate as adults' — even if the reasons for the emotions seem minor from an adult perspective. Not making the cheer-leading squad may not seem like a big deal to a parent, but you must relate it to the experience of adults who work long and hard for a promotion, and yet someone else gets the job. They know that they were better qualified, and losing the promotion hurts. Teenagers who have failed feel the same way — emotionally devastated. Don't look down on them and say, "You don't have reason to hurt," or "I have more reasons to hurt, and I'm handling it." Whether you are an adult or an adolescent, problems can hurt.

Keep in mind that everyone has a different level of tilt. Everyone is capable of committing suicide, and everyone can hurt so much that they no longer want to live. It is a fact that most people don't like to face, but there can come a time in any life, no matter how successful and content, when suicide becomes an option. To say "Your problem isn't big enough" means that you don't understand. Each person's problems and ability to deal with them are unique. Treat teens and their difficulties with respect.

5. Stay with them.
Don't leave a hurting teen alone, especially not after they've reached stage two or three. Emotionally, this person is as injured as if they had suffered a physical trauma. If they had been in a horrible car accident, they would be constantly attended to. First the ambulance and the fire department would arrive, and the patient would be stabilized. Then they would be rushed to the hospital, where they'd receive advanced life support. After stabilization the injured person would be put in intensive care for around-the-clock monitoring. Once out of intensive care they'd be transferred to a regular unit, but would remain within reach of a push-button call for help, with nurses and doctors making regular rounds. This person would be ministered to constantly. Suicidal kids are hurting so much emotionally that they need the same around-the-clock monitoring.

Get others involved so you don't have the sole responsibility of supporting the depressed teen. It is one thing to make them promise not to hurt themselves, but it is equally necessary to make sure that they are not left alone. It is not your responsibility, or within your ability, to stay with them all the time. You need to recruit others to help.

If you are the parent, talk to their friends and call their school. Speak with counselors, church members, siblings, and anyone else you feel can help and provide support. You may have promised not to tell anyone about what is happening; you don't have to relate the exact nature of the problem. You do need to build support.

It is not necessary to tell the depressed person that you've asked other people to reach out to them. They may choose to interpret that as being the only reason people care. Give them time to heal first.

6. Don't challenge the individual to act on the threat.
This may seem like common sense, but I know people who have said to someone who was feeling suicidal, "I'm sick and tired of hearing you talk about it. Why don't you just go ahead

Some depressed kids will be pushed over the brink just to prove that they are serious about their intentions. All suicide threats or attempts, no matter how "minor," should be treated seriously.

7. Keep the depressed person active.

Keep them active and keep their mind off their problems. This may appears contradictory, as we've encouraged them to talk about what caused the depression. After all, not talking is what prevented them from working the depression out when it began. But there is nothing worse for suicidal teens than being alone and staying alone. It is too easy to focus on their problems when they are by themselves.

During recovery there is a time for talking and counseling, and there is a time for getting on with daily life. Depressed kids need to get back into the real world, even if they are reluctant at first. Take them to the movies, go shopping with them, take a walk together, do anything to get them out in the world again. Consider this to be the emotional equivalent of physical therapy after an accident. It is a way of rehabilitating them into society, drawing them in again, a little bit at a time.

8. Tell them, and help them, to stay away from drugs and alcohol.

Drugs and alcohol mask problems temporarily. As Chapter 6, Drug and Alcohol Abuse, will make clear, these crutches make the user more depressed in the long run. Suicidal teens must not "self-medicate" to help themselves feel better.

If there is a recurring theme in this book, it is to love and care for one another so that depression can be overcome quickly. Be a good listener at all times, not just when someone is dangerously depressed. Be aware of the signs of depression, and above all else, be willing to reach out and help.

Questions and Answers

1. What kind of family pressures affect kids?

Whatever pressures affect mom and dad affect the kids: job transfers, layoffs, problems at work, money problems, social problems, anger between the parents, or parents' frustration with the other children. Anything that involves the parent will filter down and affect the child.

2. I feel unqualified to help. Maybe as a parent I'm too close to the situation.

You might be. Consider Rob's story in Chapter 1: the circumstances in his life were not something he was willing to share with his parents. The point to remember is that everybody gets depressed and hurts. What matters is that you find people your child can talk to, whether or not they can communicate with you. There is a sheet in the back of this book that can be used to help your child list the people they can talk to. That is their support system.

3. What if my child won't listen to me?

Join the club. The point of adolescence is to make the transition from childhood to adulthood. Somewhere along the line teens begin to think that they know more than you do, simply because that's the nature of being a teenager. When I was 17 I didn't know how my dad could function. After I was married and had kids, my dad became a very intelligent man. Your kids will go through that, too.

The way to get young people to listen to you is not by lecturing, but through discussion. You have to earn the right to be listened to. If the subject is depression, tell them that you've been hurt and that you understand what it feels like. Tell them that when they come to a point where they're emotionally hurting, you'll listen to them.

Describe to them what a sick feeling you get in the pit of your stomach when you look in the rear view mirror and see a police car with flashing lights. Let them know what it feels like to go through a romantic breakup. Share with them how you felt when someone wanted you to do something you really didn't want to do, but at the same time you didn't want to be laughed at and called a chicken. Then teenagers understand that these kinds of feelings and experiences are universal, and when they go through them they'll know you can listen.

4. I'm a good listener, but my kids won't talk.

A lot of teens won't talk because they feel that their parents won't understand or because their parents are in the habit of yelling at them. You must earn the right to be a listener.

Often kids won't talk simply because you're not really listening. Practice these good listening techniques: Don't be ready with pat answers. Acknowledge how they feel even if you don't understand it personally. Let them talk without butting in about how you'd feel or what you'd do in the same situation. Let them live their own lives, but be an interested and willing participant when they want you to be. Listen with equal respect to their difficulties at 10 years old or 12 years old, because if you tell them or indicate to them then that their problems are no big deal, they won't come to you later when their problems *are* a big deal. You must make six-year-old problems big enough, 10-year-old problems big enough, and 17-year-old problems big enough to merit your attention and care.

5. Do parents have to have the answers?

Thank goodness we don't need to have the answers to every problem. In fact, that's one thing a lot of kids complain about. When they try to talk to their parents, the parents want to provide a solution. Kids usually don't want that; they just want a sounding board.

Besides, the answers might not be available. I talk to kids all the time who are depressed, and there is no way to make the problem go away. If their parents are getting a divorce or if they are being neglected emotionally, I can't go back in time and change that. There is not an "answer" to be had. But I can help them live through those experiences. I can let them know I care and then love them through it. Parents can do the same thing.

6. How do I know when to talk and when to give my children the privacy they need?

This is a question that doesn't have a single answer. You need to trust your instincts. Adults need privacy, times alone, and times to talk. Young people do too. If kids spend too much time alone, that's not good, but don't barge into their room every time they shut the door. Each child and each family is different. You have to trust your feelings; build a relationship and communication with your child.

If you are concerned, tell them that you are available when they need to talk, or set a time to talk. I often do that with my children. If something is bothering them, I give them an hour to think it out, and then we sit down and talk. That way I've given them a time to be alone and a time to talk.

7. If someone else's child comes to me with a problem, should I tell their parents?

That depends. If the child comes to you just because they're depressed over average teenage problems — breakups, poor self-confidence, loneliness — talk to them and help them through it. Later you may want to tell their parents that you talked to their son or daughter and were able to help them out.

But if a young person tells you something that involves physical abuse, sexual abuse, drug or alcohol abuse, or pregnancy, their parents probably need to be told. (An exception is when the parent is the direct cause of the problem. Then you should go over the parent's head first.) There isn't a rule of thumb for every situation; there are just too many variables. You have to use your best judgment. Generally I try to get the parents involved when I'm working with their child. My goal is to let them know what is going on without destroying the confidentiality or trust that the child has in me.

8. We've just moved, so we're new in the area. We don't have any friends or family close by. I know it's tough on my kids; it's tough on me. How do we find support?

Do things that will help your kids build support. Get your teens involved in a church youth group, where kids come together in a smaller group than at school and where they can participate with others who share their beliefs. If your child is artistic, athletic, or musical, help them find activities with other teenagers who share those interests. Also, after they've been in school a few weeks, you might invite some of their new friends over. Make it as easy as possible.

What you don't want to do is to move and then tell your children they are on their own and wish them good luck. Being in an unfamiliar area is a difficult situation, and the key is to make it as easy as possible for your children to make friends, to rebuild their support system.

5

How to Talk to Each Other

"Bill Cosby says that when kids turn 13 they should be put in a barrel and fed through the knothole. Then when they turn 15, you should plug the knothole and not let them out until they're 18."

Bill Cosby — as quoted by Michael Miller

Gresham Union High School

When I was working at the fire department the chief called me into his office one day and said, "Michael, I want you to do me a favor."

I said, "Sure chief, anything."

He said, "I want you to go to Portland and pick something up for me."

I said, "Sure, no problem."

"Here, take my car."

I went, "Yeah!"

I loved driving the fire chief's car. The reason I liked driving it was that it was a four-door white sedan with a light bar on the roof. It had a spotlight and writing on the door. From the rear view mirror it looked just like a cop car. What I would do is go to the freeway, get *on the on-ramp, and wait for some teenage guy to go zipping down the road doing about 70. Then I'd pull out right behind him. Ever seen a teenage guy with a cop behind him? He starts sweating. Let me tell you something. (This has nothing to do with teen suicide.) Guys, I'm going to tell you how to keep from getting a ticket. I've got a friend who's a highway patrol officer, and he told me, "When I get behind a teenager and he looks in his rear view mirror and sees me, his shoulders go up and I can practically hear him say, 'Oh no, there's a cop!' As soon as his shoulders go up, I pull him over because I know he's guilty." So if you see a cop, keep your shoulders down, O.K.?*

Have you ever seen a car go from 70 to 40 in three feet? He'd change lanes. I'd change lanes. I'd make that kid sweat. Don't think I'm a bad person, because if any of you had the opportunity, you know you'd do the same thing. You'd probably park around the corner from your best friend's house and follow him.

When I present *Dare to Live* I tell funny stories. I have been criticized because people think I'm making suicide a joke; they don't like to hear students laugh when it's supposed to be a serious topic. But if I can't make kids laugh, I can't keep their attention. Swinging back and forth between the "serious stuff" and the anecdotes keeps students on the edge of their seats. They don't know when I'll break up a somber story with an irreverent remark. That is how I get them to listen. (The humor may be for the kids, but the teachers laugh just as hard.)

Then, as they listen, the real message sinks in. They leave the auditorium, gym, or classroom talking about what they've heard. The funny stories bring to mind the serious points. The serious points are firmly planted in their heads. I wouldn't get very many callbacks if the whole school left my assembly weeping.

Using humor to get a point across is just one technique I employ when talking to students. When I counsel teens who are considering suicide, I may have to try two or three different tacks to make them look honestly at their problems. Sometimes I have to get angry, sometimes logical, sometimes pragmatic. Whatever works is fair game to make kids understand depression.

But whenever I talk to kids, I come from a solid base of love. I tell them I care about them. I hug them and comfort them. Loving and caring for them works. This is what kids tell me: "I came to you instead of my parents because you let me know you cared for me."

I know that parents love their kids. Parents know that they love their kids. So why don't kids think that their parents love them? One reason may be that it is easy for adults to get caught up in the shuffle of going to work, running a household, paying the mortgage, keeping the house clean, and just surviving, unintentionally neglecting to spend the time needed to assure their children that they love them. The main problems between parents and teens seem to be communication of love and finding ways to live together so that everyone feels loved, needed, and cherished.

This chapter's purpose is to give kids and parents — as well as counselors, teachers, clergy, and other concerned adults — ways to talk to each other so that the end result is communication, not yelling, defiance, anger, or frustration. Addressing parents first and teenagers next, it applies many of the techniques and lessons I've learned while working with teenagers, including my own kids, day after day.

Part One: How to Talk to Your Kids — A Section for Parents

1. Treat your children like human beings.
Don't talk down to adolescents. They appreciate that most of all. They are persons like anyone else. Treat them with

respect. We adults are impatient and intolerant of condescension. We don't want to believe that one person is better than another person. An adult is uncomfortable in a boss/employee relationship if the boss is patronizing. Likewise, young people are uncomfortable and resentful when parents talk down to them. "You wouldn't understand." "Let me try to explain it to you." "You'll know what I'm talking about when you're older." These statements are condescending. It's no wonder that kids react with resentment. The trick is to talk to kids with maturity and wisdom, packaged so teens can understand and use the information. It is not an easy feat.

Parents tumble into two other pitfalls when trying to communicate with kids. First, adults lose perspective because the teen physically resembles an adult. Parents and teachers forget that teens are still kids; even if they look like adults, they make kid mistakes and think, sound, and act like kids.

Second, adults forget to consider a teenager's point of reference. Young people have only one point of reference: here and now. Everything known and experienced is based on their current age. If a teen is 16 years old, everything he or she has experienced on this planet is from the past 16 years. And, *whether students are 13, 15, or 19, they are more mature than they have ever been before in their lives.* So when a teen discusses an issue with mom and dad, what he says may be logical and precise, from his 16-year-old point of view and maturity level.

On the other hand, mom's and dad's perspective has changed with the years. Parents used to be 16, they used to be 18, and they used to be 21. Now they are in their 30s, 40s, or 50s, and their point of reference is greater than the teen's. An adolescent can't raise his or her point of reference or maturity level to that of an adult. A teen hasn't had adult experiences. Therefore, it is up to parents to speak to young people in such a way that they will understand. If you approach kids with the attitude that you are older, maturer, and wiser, you'll probably be condescending. If you remember the teen's point of reference, you'll better understand what they are trying to communicate.

2. Communication must grow with your children.

Another problem between parents and teens is one of changing communication needs. Ever since the teen was a baby, the parents have been in charge. They've told him or her how to dress and when to dress, when to eat and what to eat, where to go and how to do it, for so long — 13 years at least — that they have become used to being in control. When the teen was a five-year-old, parents dictated: "Go to bed. Clean your room. Get dressed." Theirs was one-sided communication.

Talking to teenagers should be conversation rather than dictation. The order, "Go to bed," has to change.

"It's time for bed."

"But I haven't finished my homework.'

"When will you be done?"

"In another half an hour."

"All right, go to bed when you're through."

This discussion is two-sided and necessary. As children become teenagers they are less like children and more like adults. As that change takes place, parents have to change their style of communication.

3. Talk at the teen's level.

When I do my assemblies, I do not aim at the mentality of an adult. Because I am talking to teenagers, I tell stories and use examples that will reach kids. I have to gear myself to that. When I speak to adults, I don't use the same stories and the same humor that I use at the schools.

As children grow, what they understand and find funny changes. For example, I have noticed an evolution of humor with my kids. In first grade my daughter Hannah loved this joke:

"You know what?"

"What?"

"That's what!"

It was the funniest thing she had ever heard. She could tell me the same joke six times in a row, and every time she'd laugh just as hard.

My son Matthew, then 10 years, was more sophisticated. Hannah would try the joke on him.

"You know what?"

"What?"

"That's what!" she'd giggle.

"That isn't funny," he'd respond. But, if he saw someone slip on a banana peel, he'd be in stitches. Slapstick humor was the height of hilarity to him. As we grow older, the things we once thought funny are no longer even amusing. This is simply a point of maturity. In the same way that humor evolves, the way we talk to our kids has to change, too.

What is the purpose of talking? It is communication. Communication is the giving and, more importantly, the receiving of information. If you talk to a person all day and they don't receive, you haven't had communication. You've just talked.

It takes a conscious effort to speak to young people in a way that they will understand. That is one reason why *Dare to Live* is successful in reaching teens. It is not only that what I have to say is important, but that kids *receive* what I'm saying because I talk to them at their level.

A parent's goal is to communicate with children in a way that they can receive. How each one receives is a matter of individuality, maturity, and openness. Each child is unique. But if parents maintain the determination to relate to their children, they will succeed. If your kids — whether toddlers or teenagers — can't relate to you, you have to relate to them.

When I was in college I took a class in ancient history. I remember the professor's lectures because he used dictionary words. I spent half my time writing down words to look up later to see what he was talking about. One day in class he was discussing the Greek god "Zayoos."

I said, "What?" I had never heard of this particular god.

The student in front of me turned around and said, "What he means is Zeus."

The professor wigged out. "I do not mean Zeus!" he yelled, "the proper pronunciation is 'Zayoos.' "

I said, "Why don't you talk so I can understand you? I paid money to be in this class. I want to receive something from it."

He glared at me and said, "It has taken me 48 years to bring my vocabulary to this level. I refuse to lower my vocabulary to your level. If you want to learn from me, you have to raise your vocabulary to mine."

To me this was the height of stupidity and arrogance. The professor wasn't interested in having students receive his knowledge. He just wanted to impress us with his 48 years of learning.

You will miss the mark in communicating if you talk over or under your child's level. Consider the 15- or 16-year-old, and remember that he or she has no greater basis of understanding than being 15 or 16. Expecting them to understand more leads to frustration for everyone. Conversely, just as you wouldn't expect a toddler to understand a discourse on mathematics, or even an episode of "Bill Cosby," you wouldn't tell your 13-year-old, "Sleepy-bye time. Nighty-night." If you talk like that, your child will be offended. Talk at the child's level.

4. Be clear and concise.

Say what you mean; mean what you say. Teens operate under the assumption that choices and decisions are black or white; to them there are no shades of gray. And under this assumption, when something happens that falls into a "gray area," the response often is "That's not fair!" When they ask a question, they want a clear answer: yes or no. They don't like to be put off. So parents have to say *exactly* what they mean. They must be clear and concise.

If I make a promise, I uphold it no matter what. If I announce a threat, I have to be prepared to follow through with the stated consequences. That means I have to be careful about what I say. If I promise to help my kids work on their fort, and then I come home and it's pouring buckets of rain, they still expect me to work on the fort. If I say, "One more time and you'll lose that privilege," I must be ready to take away the privilege when the line is crossed. I have to be specific and consistent.

There are different levels of communication: Parents communicate to kids that they are loved. They impart knowledge. They communicate when they discipline kids. They communicate when they converse with kids. In all instances parents must be clear and concise so that young people understand what their elders are talking about and feel they are being treated fairly.

5. Be loving in your communication.

As we've said, you must be clear. You need to talk at your child's level. And when you communicate with your kids, they need to understand your motive. The motive must always be love. I talk to my kids because I love them. I discipline them because I love them; I teach them because I love them. Every time I speak to them it is because I love and care for them. Kids need to know that.

Besides being loving in what you say, there are other ways to express that you care. One of my friends has a son who is 16, long, and lanky. He is in many ways a grown person. Yet he comes to his mom at nights and they have a ritual from his childhood called "dee-deeing." She gently runs her fingers over his arms, hair, or neck. This adolescent, who wouldn't be caught dead hugging his mom in front of his friends, will lie down beside her just to get his head rubbed.

This mother is communicating love. It's not verbal, but it's just as if she had said it in words. The reason he keeps coming back for more is not for the pleasure of the physical contact, but because she is showing him she loves him. There is so much uncertainty in the teenage years that kids need tons of love, support, and caring.

Doing things with your kids fosters another type of non-verbal, loving communication. My daughter Hannah and I have a special garden spot. We have planted flowers there, and every summer evening when I come home from work we go out and water the flowers. I'm not a gardener and I don't like yard work, but I do it because it is something special for Hannah and me to share.

My son Matthew is very physical. He loves to wrestle. My father didn't wrestle much with my brothers and me, so it is not a "natural" thing for me to do. Yet I do it because it is what Matthew needs and it is a way of communicating my love for him.

Everything works better with love. Conversely, nothing is accomplished when anger is the vehicle. Don't speak to your kids in anger. There was a television commercial that showed a small boy with a very sad face. The voice-over said, "Kids believe what they hear," and in the background an angry woman was yelling, "You're pathetic. You're a loser. You're no good." Do not talk to your kids like that. If you're angry and irrational, give yourself a cooling-off time. It is much easier to allow your emotions to subside than to have to later make amends for what you said or did in anger.

You have only one chance to raise your child. You can't go back when your kid is 16 and say, "I think I've messed up. Let's start over." Work on doing it right the first time.

Kids tell me, "My mom and dad hate me."

"What do you mean, they hate you?"

"They yell at me all the time. They're always grumpy because my room is messy, and they make it a big deal if I'm late, even once."

Teenagers can build a case that their parents don't like them.

If one talks to the parents, they say the opposite. They love their kids! But the communication has disintegrated from a loving exchange to an angry one. They say you can catch more flies with honey than with vinegar, but too many of us tend to turn to bitter vinegar first.

Yelling affects kids much more than many parents realize. Remember what Rob said in Chapter 1? "I didn't know that my dad's yelling was his way of caring. I just thought he was there to yell, to be a disciplinarian." Little Molly said the same thing in a different way. Listening to her mom and dad yell at her older brother and sister affected her much more than anyone in her family realized. Be careful of raised voices.

Shouting at someone doesn't mean that you don't love them, and there are times when all parents shout, but it isn't effective communication. When I yell at the people I love, my motivation is usually fear. I might be scared because my daughter is out an hour past curfew, and in that hour I'm sitting at home imagining a horrible traffic accident. My immediate response when she arrives is anger: "I don't ever want you to do that again!"

Her response may be to defend what she did and yell back at me. She returns kind for kind. "Well, I'm not promising anything," she shouts, mad because she has not been given a chance to explain her actions. "I'm old enough to make my own decisions."

At this point some parents might deride their daughter's mentality and make wild threats. But if you attack your teenager, they'll attack back, and you'll probably end up threatening them. "That's the stupidest thing I've ever heard! If you do that again you won't leave the house for a month!"

Instead of reacting with anger, try first to explain your feelings: "I get really scared when you are late. If you had been hurt or in trouble, it would have hurt me because I love you. I worry about you." This tack should better the chances that your children will listen and understand how you feel.

If you're already responding out of fear, you can't help that. For example, when children run into the street, you react out of fear for their lives. But after the fear parents can go back and explain their reaction: "When you miss your curfew I start to worry about where you are. I'm sorry I yelled, but I don't like worrying about you. I want you home when we have asked you to be, for our sanity and your safety. If you feel your curfew is too early, then let's talk about that." This way, you soothe hurt feelings and explain the motivation behind your feelings. It lets them know that you weren't yelling at them because you dislike them, but because you love them.

Similarly, you can talk about the kinds of situations that will make you angry *before* they happen. You should tell teenagers, "Look, I don't want you to go out and drink. But if you end up in a situation where you've been drinking and you have to get home, by all means call me. Will I be upset? Yes, I'll be upset, but I'd much rather you called for a ride than have you drive yourself home drunk and get hurt. I'm telling you this because I love you." Everything has to be reinforced with love. Kids know that parents are going to get mad, but if they understand that the anger is because their parents love and care for them, it is easier to accept.

This leads to the question of punishment and how to tie it to communication with love. The purpose of punishment is to reinforce the point that the child exhibited negative behavior. Yet even punishment has to be meted out in love.

Different punishments work for different people. For some kids, groundings or time-outs work; for others they don't. Parents need to find what works for their children. My oldest daughter only has to be spoken to and she is contrite. My second daughter, when given a time-out, throws herself a pity party. I can't leave her alone because she ends up feeling sorrier for herself than for her behavior. I have to sit down and talk with her about her wrongdoings.

My son is immune to time-outs, but if I tell him to get the

paddle, the punishment is effective. Corporal punishment is not for everyone, and I never use it when I'm angry. My dad used to spank me in anger, and it didn't work. All I could think about was showing him that he couldn't hurt me. For my son, the paddle is an attention-getter. It is a message from me that his transgression is serious.

Grounding doesn't work for the son of some friends of mine. It makes him angry and resentful. So when he breaks the rules, his father imposes a monetary penalty. "Todd, for borrowing the car without asking, you are fined $30. If you want to work off the $30, you can weed the front flower bed, and then you will be free to go out tonight." Todd hates yard work, but he has been given a choice and a chance to "pay" for breaking the rules. This is effective punishment and effective loving communication.

6. Sometimes it isn't what you say but how you say it.

Listen to *how* you speak to young people, not just what words come out of your mouth. Matthew, my son, brought this point home to me loud and clear one night.

Matthew was about 10 years old at the time and not very interested in his personal hygiene. Frankly, too many other things were more important to him, so I was on his case all the time.

"Matt, when was the last time you brushed your teeth?"

"Matt, comb your hair."

"Matt, change your clothes."

I kept saying his name in an exasperated, long-suffering tone of voice.

One night as I was tucking him into bed, Matt looked up at me and said, "Dad, I'm sorry I'm so stupid."

I got mad. I thought someone at school was calling him names. "What do you mean? You're not stupid! Who's said you were stupid?"

"You did, dad."

"Matt, I've never said you were stupid!"

"Dad, you say I'm stupid all the time."

"When?"

"Just the way you say my name makes me feel stupid."

It was as if he had stabbed me in the heart. I went to bed and cried. What was I doing? I was trying to help all these kids, but what was I doing to my own son?

I stopped putting him down and started building him up. I went out of my way to say, "Good job, Matt. All right, Matt." I have not ever used his name in that exasperated tone of voice again. If he's doing something wrong I'll say, "Matt, let me show you a better way to do that." Or, "Matt, don't you think you ought to brush your teeth?" Instead of being negative I've tried to make everything I tell him positive. This is the least I can do for my child.

7. Open the doors to communication.

Another thing that parents overlook doing, because it seems so obvious, is to give their children permission to talk to them about their problems. I have always encouraged my kids to come to me when they are hurting or confused, and it has paid off many times. Not only do they come to me, but often they send their friends, too.

When my oldest daughter was on the threshold of her teen-age years I was inundating her with verbal assurances of my love and support. I was building a fortress of love to shelter her in as her life became more exciting and scary. One day she came to me and said, "You know how you've told me, dad, that if ever you were doing something that bothered me I should tell you about it?"

"Sure, honey, I remember that."

"Well, daddy, you're doing something that's bothering me."

"What's that?" I asked.

"Daddy, I think you are telling me that you love me more often than you're telling the others."

She had come to me since she felt we had a problem and she cared about the feelings of her younger brothers and sisters enough to worry about getting too much love from me. This tells me that I have been successful in showing and teaching loving communication.

Part Two: How to Talk to your Parents — A Section for Teens

Gresham Union High School

B*abies are basically born as lumps. I've said it earlier: they eat, sleep, cry, mess, and stink. After two years of that, they become toddlers. Toddlers have only one thing on their minds, and that is how to hurt themselves in the most ingenious manner possible. They'll play in the middle of the street. They'll skydive off a refrigerator. They have no mental concept of danger.*

Did you ever know a two-year-old?

"It's quiet. What are they up to now?" You just know they're doing something destructive.

A two-year-old becomes a three-year-old. A three-year-old has a two-word vocabulary: "Why?" and "No!"

"It's time to go to bed."

"Why?"

"Because the sun went down."

"Why?"

"Because it's night."

"Why?"

"Because the sun passed through the heavens and set in the west!"

"Why?"

"Because — God — Made — It — That — Way!"

"Why?"

"HE DIDN'T TELL ME! GO TO BED!!!"
"No."
You cannot carry on a logical conversation with a three-year-old. A three-year-old becomes a four-year-old. Four-year-olds have one thing on their minds: "You know I get to go to kindergarten? Next year I get to go to kindergarten! I get to ride the big yellow school bus! I get to carry a lunch box! I get to go to school next year!"
Then what happens? They turn five. They go to the first day of school. The next day their mother wakes them up and says, "It's time to go to school."
"What? You mean I have to go back?"
After that, parents spend the next 12 years of their lives ripping their kids out of bed. Ask yourself as a teenager, logically, would you have made it this far in school if your parents hadn't made you get out of bed most mornings? No, you wouldn't. You would have dropped out in third grade.
Would you even have teeth right now if your parents didn't say, "Did you brush your teeth? Did you brush your teeth? Go brush your teeth."
If you give an eight-year-old the choice, "Do you want Twinkies and Pepsi for dinner, or do you want broccoli?" they take the Twinkies and Pepsi every time. You'd be a dropout, unhealthy, not have a tooth in your head, and be a shell of what you are now without your parents.
Your parents have done all that for you, and the way you've repaid them is by becoming a teenager. Now, in becoming a teenager, you have to realize that it is hard for your parents to see you grow up, and it's hard for you to grow up. There has to be change on both sides. But the key to change is communication.

Every teenager I talk to is an individual with his or her own personality and problems. But there are themes and statements I hear over and over, especially about communication with parents. Let's hear from the teens now.

1. "My parents wouldn't understand."

One thing kids forget to think about when they talk to parents is that parents were once teenagers themselves. Kids don't remember this because all the time that their kids have known them the parents have been adults. Teens figure that their parents were always adults and that as adults they can't comprehend what teenagers go through.

Believe it or not, parents can and will understand your feelings. Parents were teenagers too. They got in trouble, went on dates, had girlfriends and boyfriends dump them, fought with their folks, and had to deal with peer pressure. Kids are going through nothing that their parents have not also experienced.

It helps to maintain a mental picture of your parents as teenagers. If you remember that your parents once went through the same things that you are experiencing now, then maybe it is possible to go to them when you need help. After all, being an adolescent is what a parent had to go through to become a parent. (But some parents do lose perspective of what it is like to be a teen. We covered that in the first half of this chapter.)

2. "My parents are going to kill me!"

Let's be honest. Parents generally don't go around killing their children. It is counterproductive. They don't go through the agony of giving birth, changing diapers, shoveling in baby food, and buying thousands of dollars worth of school supplies so they can murder their offspring. They've invested too much money to kill them. Parents might want to give their kids away or sell them into slavery, but they just don't kill their children.

Generally, the worst thing that will happen when you get in trouble is that you will get yelled at. You have this fear of getting yelled at, but you get yelled at all the time anyway. It may be hard to believe, but parents yell because they love you. They care about what happens to you. Wouldn't it be better to deal with the problem and to accept the consequences than to let it linger and to go through the agony and emotional trauma of wondering when it will all cave in on your head?

Since it is you, the teenager, who is having the problem, it becomes your responsibility to pick the time to communicate with your parents about the situation. Pick your time well. Instead of springing the bad news on your folks at an inopportune moment — say when they are paying the bills or entertaining the boss — pick a time you can really talk.

Start off by saying, "Mom and dad, I need to talk to you. When would be a good time? Let's set up a time that is convenient for both of us." Most parents will drop whatever they are doing because this mature approach lets them know the subject is important to you.

Come to them openly and honestly, and give them the full truth. It is silly to withhold information because you don't think it is relevant or important; it might be very relevant in your parents' eyes. If you hold back they will think that you've withheld other information or that they are being manipulated. Parents don't like to be manipulated by their children any more than you like to be manipulated by your friends. If your folks find out the complete truth later, you'll have to go through the whole process again and they will be mad all over again. Reveal everything immediately.

Usually whatever happened will eventually come out anyway, so make the first move. Tell them you've done wrong and admit to your mistakes. Parents want their kids to be honest and trustworthy, and confession will help build trust between you and your parents.

Mistakes will be made as you grow up, as well as throughout your adult life. But don't take for granted that because you're young it's O.K. to make mistakes instead of trying to act responsibly. I've heard a lot of kids say, "It's O.K. for me to blow it; I'm a kid." No. It is never all right to make mistakes if you're making them because you don't care enough to do your best in each situation. The point of growing up is not seeing how many mistakes you can get away with. The point of growing up is to learn from your mistakes so that you don't do the same thing time and time again.

If you get a speeding ticket, for example, take that as a lesson that when you speed, you'll get caught and have to pay a fine. Don't figure that since you sped 10 times and were only caught once, you can speed nine more times. Sooner or later you'll lose your driver's license or have an accident. A penalty will have to be paid. Mistakes cost. Sometimes the price is very high.

But remember, even if you've made a really big mistake, your parents will still love you. Just give them a little time to work through their other emotions first.

3. "You don't know my parents — it's impossible to talk to them."

It's true. I don't know your parents personally, but I know parents and parenting in general. Teens tell me that when they sit down to talk to their parents they start off by saying, "Mom, dad, this is how I'm feeling." Then the parents take over the situation because they are used to doing that. They've done it ever since you were a little child.

Let's look at the situation: You've just shared a problem with them and suddenly they are telling you how you think, why you think it, and when you'll stop thinking that way. Then they'll tell you what you will do about it, how you'll do it, and when. You just shut up. What else can you do?

Parents do tend to take over because they are used to taking care of you. If you approach your folks to talk and they take charge of the conversation, it closes the door on communication. (You might give this book back to them and ask them to read the first part of this chapter more carefully, especially the section on changing communication.) It is hard to talk when someone isn't interested in listening to you. Without losing your temper, you need to ask again if you can say something.

If you have really stubborn parents who still cut you off, there are steps you can follow to reopen communication. Many kids do have to go this far, because a lot of parents automatically take over. Teens who have tried the following steps say they work.

If you feel you have not been able to plead your case, try writing them a letter using the following guidelines.

Start your letter or note by telling them what they want to hear. "Mom and dad, you are my parents and I will always love you. I care about you and I know that you've been good parents." You want them to know that you realize how hard they work to support you. You love them for that. Showing them love and respect are their just desserts for being your parents.

Next, write down your grievances. Include how you felt when you tried to talk to them, but do it in such a way that they will be impressed by your mature approach and be open-minded to your problems. Parents are adult and mature, so you, the teenager, have to approach them in an adult and mature manner.

Then present the problem or request. You've come to them in an adult manner that they can respond to; now communicate the situation. "I think you yelled at me unjustly," or, "You grounded me for the rest of my natural life and I think that's too long." State your grievance simply and concisely. End the letter by telling your folks that you love and care for them and asking for a time to talk about the problem.

The advantage to writing is that when a person gets a letter, they read all of it — unlike a phone call that they can hang up on or a conversation that they can interrupt. They may disagree with or get angry over what is in your letter, but they will read the whole thing.

It is important to give them the letter at a time when they can digest the information and look at it from your point of view. Give it to them in the morning when you're leaving for school and they have six or seven hours to think about it. Even if they are initially angry or upset, their first reaction will fade and they will begin considering the contents logically. When you get back together, ask again for a time to discuss the subject of your letter.

Remember, communication is for good times as well as difficult times. Don't come to your parents only when you have a gripe. Talk to them when everything's great. Share your victories, too. Don't make them drag it out of you. Volunteer the information that you got a high score on your math test or did well at basketball practice. Parents are nosy only because they love you and want to be part of your life. If you volunteer the details before they ask, they will probably ask fewer questions. Should you have problems talking face to face to your mom and dad even when the subject is pleasant, write a note telling them about the positive events in your life.

However you approach them, don't look at your parents as bad guys who will only say "no" when you ask if you can shave your head and tattoo a butterfly on your scalp. If they say "no" don't think, "My parents never let me do anything fun." Maybe in the future you'll be glad they put their foot down. Maybe they have a little more wisdom and insight into life than you do. You don't have to agree with them. You do need to respect them and follow their wishes.

Communication has to be ongoing; it needs to be learned and practiced daily. After all, communication — talking or writing — is the only way you're going to get anything across to your parents. Arguing, shutting yourself in the bedroom, and playing music really loud is not going to accomplish anything. Try, and try again, to really talk to your parents. You may be surprised by the positive results.

4. "All my parents care about is my grades."

Through junior high and high school, your mission is education. Often the issue of education causes the most difficulties between parents and teenagers. Kids feel they are doing their best, but that their best is not good enough for their parents, who seem only to focus on what is wrong with the grades and not what is right.

But after talking to thousands of students, I have a lot of

sympathy for parents. No wonder they worry: I have heard kids say that they don't want to waste too much time on school because their teenage years are when they are supposed to have fun.

That is simply not true. You are supposed to have fun all through your life. Don't dedicate your teenage years to "fun" and use that as an excuse to do poorly in school. You're supposed to have fun in your twenties and in your thirties. You should plan on having fun when you are 40, 50, 60, and even 100.

If you decide that all the fun in your life has to happen between the ages of 13 and 19, something will suffer. If it is your school work that suffers, then when you turn 18 and conclude it is time to get serious and figure out what you want from life, it may be a little late. Work on your schooling throughout your junior high and high school years. Don't cut off your options.

To help you stay focused on why you are going to school, keep a clear picture in your mind of what you want to do and be 10 years from now. How much money do you want to make? Do you want a car? What kind? Where do you want to live? How much money will you have to earn to fulfill all your expectations? If it will take an income of $40,000 a year, you'll probably need a college education. No one will pay you $40,000 to work behind the counter at McDonald's.

If you plan ahead and shoulder responsibility for your future while you are in school, you will go much farther. It is your responsibility to go to class, do your homework, and study. Your parents care a lot about your grades because they want you to have a strong foundation with plenty of options from which to choose.

Studying hard brings an added benefit. If your parents see you handling responsibility in school, they will give you more freedom and treat you more like an adult. After all, your goal is to become an adult, and the definition of an adult is someone who can handle responsibility. Remember this: You become an

adult, not when you turn 18, but when you handle the responsibilities of life.

If you are the kind of teen who works hard and does well in
school, but your parents still seem to focus only on that part of
your life, talk to them about it. Tell your folks that it feels as if
the only thing they value you for is your grade point average.
Often parents lose sight of the whole person because they are
proud of your accomplishments and want very much for you to
do better than they have. Letting them know how that kind of
pressure feels is the best way to get their understanding.

5. "My parents don't ever believe what I say."

I've talked about communicating with your parents by sitting
down and talking, or by writing a letter. There are other ways to
communicate too. Have you heard the saying, "Actions speak
louder than words?" Let's say you asked to change your curfew
from midnight to 12:30 and your parents compromised on
12:15 — but you came in at 12:30 anyway. You've shown
maturity in your ability to communicate, but immaturity in
your actions and your ability to live by your word. Actions are
a form of communication, too.

You own nothing more valuable than your word. Your word
is established as your bond by doing what you say you'll do,
being where you say you'll be, and following directions. If you
give your word, keep your word. Few things kids do feel worse
for a parent than having their child say, "I promise" when the
parent can't believe the promise.

If your word isn't worth anything because of past problems,
you can change that. Start now. If you tell your parents you'll
be in by midnight, be there — even if the car breaks down, all
four wheels fall off, you get shot six times, and are kidnapped
and drugged. If you can't be there, at least notify them. If your
dad says, "Cut the grass," cut it without 14 excuses about why
you couldn't do it. Just do it. Your word is your bond.

Building, or rebuilding, your parents' trust is a slow process, but it will reward you with a better relationship and more

freedom. By doing what you say you will do, you let your folks know you are a trustworthy person — a person who can be given more responsibility because you handle it well.

If you don't try, if you make the same mistakes over and over, your parents will feel they are being manipulated. Don't use your parents. If you want to be treated like an adult, act like an adult. The time to learn adult behavior is as a teenager.

Communication entails not only talking and writing letters but also keeping your word and handling the responsibilities you are given. If you can handle responsibility, you will receive more responsibilities and privileges in the future. Communication is giving your parents love and respect, and getting love and respect back. Tell your parents that you love them. They need to hear that from you as much as you need to hear it from them.

How to Talk to Your Parents: The Nitty-Gritty

Communication is a personal matter. Find out what works best for you and your folks. These are *your* parents. You know how to talk to them. But in case you are having problems, here are some rules for effective communication.

Look directly at your parents when you are speaking to them. Sometimes adults think you are hiding something, even if you aren't, because you don't make eye contact.

Listen attentively. Respond to what they are saying. Ask questions if necessary, but don't make them repeat themselves because your mind was wandering.

Don't raise your voice. Yelling is a way to make sure nothing gets accomplished. When your parents yell at you, you become defensive. They feel the same way when you yell at them. It is hard to think logically about a problem when emotions are hot and everyone is shouting. If you approach the problem honestly, calmly, and with maturity, your parents will respond more openly.

Sit down before you talk and prepare what you want to say.

If you have four points to make, jot down notes. That's why so many kids write letters. They can communicate more perfectly what's in their hearts by writing than by saying it verbally.

Stick to the subject. Don't regress and talk about something that happened last week or last year, unless it has direct bearing on today's problem.

There are other ways to communicate to your parents. Compose a song and sing it to them. Write them a poem. Draw them a picture. Express yourself in any way you can.

The key to changing any situation is communication. The skills that you learn at home with your parents will carry through to all parts of your life. You will have better luck communicating with your teachers, bosses, spouse, and even your own kids. (And they won't believe that you were once a kid just like them.) Good communication skills will come in handy all your life.

Parents love kids and kids love parents. It seems like such a simple thing, but in the course of growing up, problems arise. Address the issues early and together. Don't let them get out of hand. Parents and children need to be there for each other. Consider what life would be like without your family and treasure the time you have together. Communicate. Love each other.

Questions and Answers:
Parents

1. You tell me to remember what it's like being a teen, but times have changed.

Society has changed, but adolescence hasn't changed. Certainly you remember the fear of not being accepted, the horror of having a zit on the end of your nose, the confusion about sex, the concern over who liked who, worry about not being invited to a party, and terror of moving and losing your friends. All those experiences remain the same.

The teenage years are the most uncertain time in a person's life. What kids have known as childhood "norms" are changing — their bodies, their personality, the way they think, and their emotions. Everything is different than it was. We parents need to realize this and to try to remember those times so we can help guide our kids through them.

2. Can I force my child to talk?

No, you can't force anybody to talk. If you try to force teens, they'll say, "Yeah, yeah, sure, sure," and then go on their way. Kids will say what they think you want to hear so they can continue doing what they want to do. That is not communication.

Young people tell me that the main reason they don't talk to parents is because their parents won't listen to them. You have to give people the opportunity to express themselves. Communication is giving and receiving. It's an exchange of ideas and information. If communication is one-sided ("Let me tell you what is going on"), then it is a lecture. Kids quickly tune out a lecture. To begin communication you must give your child a reason to want to talk.

3. How do you get a child to talk? What will make my teenager want to talk?

Begin by making it worth their while. For instance, if a teenager wants to go out with friends, tell them they may do so *if* they sit down and have a talk with you first. Make your relationship with them the issue of these talks. Parents have to build this relationship before they can build communication. Young people need to know where you are coming from, what you think, what you feel, and why you feel that way. They need to understand how and why you make rules.

Kids will also talk if you ask for their advice and input. Then when they've come up with an idea, ask them how they made that decision. This teaches them to make decisions as an adult would.

Lots of parents also ask their teenagers to help with family rules and projects. When teens are in on the planning stages, they feel more a part of the family situation, and they better understand what it takes to reach a decision. You don't have to worry about young people being too easy on themselves. Kids are usually tougher than parents would be because they have a keen sense of fairness.

If communication has shut down entirely and you want to get your teenager to talk to you, an extreme but effective method is to get someone else to plead each side's case. Find a relative or friend whom both parents and children are comfortable with and trust to act as the mediator, referee, and arbitrator. This works because neither the parents nor the child have hostilities toward the third party. This unbiased person can understand both sides and present each side's case to the other.

I helped one family by acting as a mediator when they were unable to communicate with their daughter. Communication started with the teen in one room, her parents in the other, and me carrying messages back and forth. Eventually the girl and her parents met in the same room, and I acted as a mediator to call foul and to keep the group on the subject. Finally they began talking to each other without my help.

The purpose of all these suggestions is to get teenagers to communicate or negotiate. Get them to open up and talk about what is wrong in their lives and what is bothering them. Be creative. It doesn't matter what you do as long as communication happens.

4. How do we get past hostility?

The best way to get past hostility is to begin communicating when there is not an issue to be hotly contested. You first need to talk about being able to talk instead of going straight to the issue, be it poor grades or a messy room.

Both persons also have to realize that they want to talk and that communication must take place. If one person wants to talk but the other person doesn't, nothing will happen. If you can't get past hostility by talking, write a letter. Let your children know how you feel. Tell them that you love them and care how they are thinking and feeling. Do whatever it takes to begin communication.

5. When is the best time to talk to my children?

The best situation is uninterrupted and focused. It is when nobody is tired, distracted, or already upset about something else. When your child comes in half an hour after curfew and you're mad, it is not a good time to talk. The most conducive time to talk is when you can make it as positive as possible.

The best time is one that is convenient for everyone. If your child is a night owl and you are an early bird, don't wake the kid at 7 a.m. on Saturday for a talk.

Pick a time that is unhurried. To ensure this, make an appointment. Be well prepared. Write a list of the things that are bothering you, or set an agenda — after all, agendas are used in the business world to make sure all the important topics are covered. Stick with the agenda.

These suggestions are for times when there is an issue to be discussed or resolved. You certainly don't have to set up appointments and agendas for spontaneous talks.

6. How should I handle a situation in which my children's actions make me so mad I could strangle them?

Don't deal with your children when you're that mad. Ask them to go to their room, or go to your own room and cool off. Then after you're calmer deal with it. Yelling will not solve the problem. When you're angry you can't be rational or accomplish anything positive. Count to 10, say the alphabet backward — whatever it takes to cool off — but try not to deal with your children when you're angry.

7. Why would my kids want to talk to someone else instead of to me?

It may be that you are the problem. Or they may need to tell their problems to someone else. That's O.K.; there is nothing wrong with that. I'm sure there have been situations in your life that you never discussed with your parents. So it will be between you and your children.

8. Who else should I tell my kids to talk to?

Include other family members, your kids' friends, their friends' parents, teachers, clergy, and neighbors. The information in Chapter 4 on where to go for help should be read by all young people from age 10 up. In addition, there is a work sheet in the back of the book that can be copied or torn out so that each teen can make a support list. Parents need to sit down with their children and help them determine their network of support.

9. How do I balance being an authority and a friend?

Your first role is always that of a parent, which means you are the authority — the person who makes the rules and metes out punishment when the rules are broken. You aren't going to be your child's best friend until they're grown.

That doesn't mean you can't love your kids, play with them, and have fun with them. But children can find friends anywhere. They only have two parents. You have to maintain your role as the authority.

10. How do I handle other kids being mean to my daughter? She comes home and tells me about the nasty things her friends are doing to her.

The first thing to do is to educate her. I've told my children that the world can be a hurtful place and that there are going to be people who do and say mean things. But I don't believe in revenge. To retaliate meanness for meanness will escalate the problem.

It also helps to teach young people how to determine whether or not someone is really a friend. They need to ask themselves if a person who puts them down and is mean is really a friend. When teens have problems like this, parents need to double their effort and give lots of positive strokes about the child's strong points. When teenagers are being pulled down in one area of their life, you have to build them up in other areas.

Also let your kids know that you will go to bat for them. If the situation can be rectified, do it. At times I've called meetings for all our neighborhood kids, passed out cookies and Kool-Aid, and told the whole group that I have heard them being mean to each other, that it is not right, and that they must stop now. I let the kids know how I feel about their behavior and why. It makes a difference.

11. What if my kids tell me something I don't want to know?

If your children tell you things you don't want to hear, that's life. Be thankful that your kids are confiding in you. No one said being a parent would be easy. We are the adults; we are grown and emotionally mature. The child is still growing. We're going to have to handle it for those who can't. If your kids tell you something really devastating, you are going to hurt too, but get support for yourself later. For now, you must be your child's support, so put the child first and be concerned about his or her feelings.

Questions and Answers:
Teens

1. What if my parents want to know more than I want to tell them?

Parents always want to know more. Even now my parents want to know more than I want to tell. You have to remember that parents want to know everything because they love you, they care, and they want to be involved in your lives. That is a compliment.

If your parents didn't love you, they wouldn't care what you thought, what you felt, or where you were going. You'd be surprised at the number of teens I talk to whose parents don't care. They wish their parents wanted to be involved in their lives.

On the other hand, you are an individual; you're a private person with your own thoughts and feelings. You can't be an open book. There will be things that you won't feel like communicating to your parents. But don't ever halt communication entirely because of issues you don't feel like sharing.

Another thing to think about is this: A lot of times the reason we don't want to tell our parents about something we are doing is that we know it is wrong. We know they will disapprove, because it really is not good for us. Consider: If you can't talk to your parents about it, should you really be doing it?

2. I'd feel like a "narc" if I told on a friend or sibling.

I do not know a single teenager who hasn't been sworn to silence about something. You should take the issue of trust seriously, but we have to look at disclosing for what it really is. You have to figure out what you're disclosing and why. If a friend tells you he borrowed his folks' car, dented it, and is sure he'll be killed when his dad finds out, there's nothing you can do to change the situation, and nothing will be gained by reporting it. On the other hand, if a friend tells you she is pregnant and plans to run away from home because her parents will kill her if they find out, she is in a dangerous situation and needs help. In this case the purpose of disclosing is to get that help. If you care, if you want to prevent friends from hurting themselves, or if you need to get them help, by all means disclose. If disclosure would get someone in trouble or stir things up, keep your mouth shut.

Never keep a serious secret bottled up inside, because then you will carry that baggage for the rest of your life. What if your pregnant friend decides to run away from home, disappears, and you never hear from her again? What if a friend says he wants to die, swears you to secrecy, and then commits suicide? You'll have to carry the burden of "what-if-you-had-told" for the rest of your life. There is merit to being honest, trustworthy, and keeping a confidence, but there is a point at which a true friend will break a promise to help a friend. It takes wisdom to know the difference.

Will your friends be upset if you "narc"? Yes, they will. I have had teens get mad at me for talking to someone I felt could help them. But they come back later and thank me. If you are a true friend and have told a secret because it was in your friend's best interest, when it is all over they'll know that what you've done is for the best.

3. Should I tell my parents about something that happened in the past and is resolved?

That depends on whether or not the issue is truly resolved. I know a lot of teens who have experienced trauma in their lives, and although time has passed, the issues are not resolved. For example, if a person was sexually abused a long time ago and the abuser is no longer around, one might think there is nothing that can be done about it. But that person is still carrying around the weight of the abuse and needs to talk about it.

If the issue is that you went to a party three years ago and got drunk, nothing can be done to change the situation. But if you are still worrying about it, talk to someone. Talking about it is one of the healthiest things you can do.

4. How do I build my parents' trust in me?

A little bit at a time. Perhaps you're the oldest in your family and your parents have never had a 15-year-old before.

Or perhaps you are the second or third child in your family, and your older brothers or sisters really messed up. Now it's your turn and your parents are really putting restrictions on you. If your parents don't trust you, ask them what you have to do to earn their trust.

Your parents want to trust you. Because you will grow up and become an adult eventually, you want responsibility, but you have to earn your folks' trust gradually. That can be accomplished by doing what you say you will do, being where you are supposed to be, and telling your parents immediately if you are not able to keep your word. Then trust will grow.

5. My parents are involved in things that I know are wrong. How can I talk to them about that?

This is a difficult situation because your parents are still the authorities. To tell them they are wrong will be difficult for you and difficult for them to respond to. It is the same as when the police, or a judge are wrong. To be the person who brings wrongdoing to the attention of authority figures is never easy, but you must talk to your folks about how you feel.

Write a letter. If you try to address the problem verbally, they may deny it. In a letter you can describe what is going on, why you think they are wrong, and how their actions affect you. Include dates, times, inconsistencies, and anything else that pertains to the problem. Your folks will sit down, read it, and hopefully look at your viewpoint logically. The only way to show a parental authority figure that they are mistaken is to communicate clearly, logically, and with love.

6

Drug and Alcohol Abuse

"Although the world is full of suffering,
it is also full of the overcoming of it."
— Helen Keller

Gresham Union High School

I grew up in a small town in southern Michigan named Detroit. Friendly little place. I had my nose broken four times before I was 16. Nice neighborhood. But when I started seventh grade I had a really good friend named Dennis Barlow. Now, Dennis was my best friend.`He had flaming red hair. We're not talking auburn; we're talking match stick. And Dennis was the type of guy who would do anything for you. He was my buddy.

Let me tell you a story. This will give you insight into Dennis. When I was in eighth grade my mom sent me down to the store to get some milk. I was walking to the store, and down around the corner lived the O'Days. They had two sons, Butch and Mark. Butch was my age and Mark was a year younger.

I walked around the corner, and Mark had a little four-year-old kid named Jeffrey out there. Jeffrey was crying. The reason he was crying was that he was trying to get away from Mark. Every time he would get up to run away, Mark would kick his feet out from under him and he would fall down and skin his knee. What a sleaze bucket, that Mark. Jeffrey'd get up; Mark would kick his feet out again. Mark was laughing and Jeffrey was crying.

In the neighborhood I grew up in, you didn't walk up and say, "Do you want to fight?" Wasn't said. So I just walked up to Mark and punched him on the back of the head. Boom. Mark fell down. Jeffrey got up and ran off.

Well, Butch was watching Mark pick on Jeffrey, and he saw me hit Mark. He came running out of the house, grabbed me, and he and I started fighting. Mark was lying over there, still out from my punch. I grabbed Butch by the hair and yanked his head back. He was saying, "AAAAaah," so I reached over to the flower bed, got a handful of black dirt, and stuck it in his mouth.

About that time Mrs. O'Day pulled into the driveway. Mark was lying on the sidewalk holding his head, Butch was making mud, and she started yelling at me, telling me I was a juvenile delinquent and was going to have my picture in every post office by the time I turned 15. I said, "Hey, wait a minute. These guys were picking on a little four-year-old."

She denied it. "My sons wouldn't do that."

I went on to the store. When I returned home my dad was there and he was hot because Mr. O'Day had called him. The one thing my dad didn't like was to have someone in the neighborhood call him up and tell him his sons were rotten. He didn't like that at all. So my dad took the board of education and applied it to the seat of knowledge until I had a bright rosy glow about the whole idea.

This was in the summer and it got dark by 9:30. About 10 o'clock that night I was sitting out on the porch and Dennis came over.

"What you doing, man?" Dennis asked. I told him what happened with the O'Days and how I got in trouble.

"What should we do about it?"

"Let's go get 'em."

"O.K., OK., you got it. Let's go!" Dennis was really excited. "What are we going to do?"

"I've got a plan," I said.

I got a couple of eggs out of the refrigerator and gave them to Dennis, saying, "Dennis, I'm going to scare the O'Days. When Mr. O'Day comes running by, you hit him with the eggs so I can get away."

"You got it, Mike, you got it! Uh-huh, uh-huh."

So we went down to the O'Day's house. Dennis hid behind a bush, and I walked up to the front window. Their drapes were open, and because it was hot they had the windows open too. I looked in the window, and Mr. and Mrs. O'Day were watching television. The lights were turned off and only the dim light from the television lit the room. They had a bowl of popcorn. Mrs. O'Day was holding the bowl.

I took the flashlight and stuck it under my chin. Then I turned it on. You know how the light comes on and it looks all scary? Mrs. O'Day looked up, saw this ghoulish face in the window, and she screamed and threw the popcorn clear across the room.

Mr. O'Day jumped up and yelled, "Don't move!"

I wasn't listening to him. I was already running. "Feet, let's go, let's go!"

Mr. O'Day came out of the gate, Dennis hit him with the eggs, and then Mr. O'Day grabbed both of us. He dragged us down the block. He had me with one arm and Dennis with the other arm, and he had egg running down the front of his face. Boy, my dad was hot. He was upset. But that was Dennis. He was my friend.

Now, Dennis Barlow came from a crummy home. I had never been to Dennis's home when his mom and dad weren't fighting. They fought constantly. When Dennis was in eighth grade, his dad pulled a $5 bill from his pocket, shoved it at Dennis and said, "Get out of here. I'm sick of looking at you, kid." Dennis left home and was gone for three days and two nights. When he came back his parents didn't even bother to ask where he had been.

Dennis hurt. By seventh grade Dennis found a way of dealing

with the rejection from his family and the hurt he was feeling. Dennis's way of dealing with rejection was to smoke dope. But in seventh grade he only smoked once or twice a week. I remember asking him, "Dennis, why are you doing this?"

I'll never forget what he answered. He looked at me and said, "Mike, I do it because it makes me feel better." I was only in seventh grade, and I didn't know how to respond to him.

By ninth grade Dennis was smoking dope before school, during school, and after school. He was getting high all the time. Then between ninth and tenth grade Dennis picked up a heroin addiction. At our school that wasn't at all hard to do.

The high school we went to had a major drug problem. Police officers in uniform would come to the school, stop you and say, "Roll up your sleeves." If they found tracks you'd be expelled from school until you went to a drug rehab program.

Right before Christmas I walked into the school bathroom and Dennis was in there. He jumped. "Oh, Mike, you scared me."

I said, "What's going on, Dennis?"

"Is anybody coming?"

"No, nobody is coming."

"Keep a watch."

"All right, but what's going on?"

"You just keep a watch for me." I should mention that the only reason Dennis came to school in tenth grade was to deal drugs to support his own habit.

I watched Dennis go to the sink, put some water in a spoon, put some powder in the spoon, and take out two matches and cook it. He took his syringe, filled it up, and I was thinking, "Dennis, you're going to stick that in your arm. You're going to leave tracks. You're going to get caught and you're going to go to a drug program. I hope they catch you today, because that would be the best thing that could happen to you."

But Dennis didn't roll up his sleeve. He tricked me. He stood in front of the mirror, opened his mouth, curled up his tongue, and injected himself in the large vein that runs underneath the tongue.

Shocked, I asked, "Dennis, why are you doing this?"

As Dennis's eyes started to cloud, he stepped back from the sink and sat down on one of the toilets. He looked up at me and said, "Mike, I do this because it makes me feel good." And he closed the stall door.

I walked out of that bathroom. I didn't go to the drug officer or the drug counselor. I didn't go to a teacher or my parents. I didn't say a word to anyone about Dennis.

Three months later — March — it was still really cold in Detroit. Monday morning, everybody showed up at school, and Dennis was dealing drugs as usual. The first-period bell rang and everybody went to class — except Dennis.

Dennis walked out of the school building, out into the parking lot, found an unlocked car, and sat down in the front seat. In the front seat of that car Dennis shot up, overdosed, and he died.

Thursday was the funeral. His mom and dad didn't even bother to come. But lots of kids from school showed up. Most of them were crying — both guys and gals — and saying what a tragic accident it had been. What a horrible way to go. Poor Dennis was only 16. Such a terrible accident.

You know, it wasn't until years later that I realized Dennis didn't die from an accident. Dennis committed suicide. Dennis hurt because of the rejection he felt from his family. What he tried to do was to cover and cover that hurt with drugs and alcohol until finally the cover became a hell itself. That March morning Dennis probably asked, "What am I even doing here?" He took his life.

Let me tell you something, young people. The world tells you that if you have a problem the way to face it is chemically. But I'm here to tell you that you cannot get drunk enough, high enough, or stoned enough to make your problems go away, because every time you come back to being sober, those problems will still be there. The only way to face your problems is sober and head-on.

Drugs and Alcohol: What Are they Doing to Us?

Drug and alcohol abuse kills this country's citizens — including teenagers — in growing numbers. Those it doesn't kill outright are often maimed physically and emotionally. Dennis's story is not unusual, and in the years I've worked with kids I've witnessed and heard many similar stories. Drugs and alcohol are a way out of life, a way to avoid reality. Too often that path leads straight to the grave. The abuse of drugs and alcohol is a subject that we must take seriously, and we cannot overemphasize to our children the importance of avoiding such abuse. The price paid is too high for too many.

How People Get "Hooked"

There are many misconceptions about how people get "hooked" on drugs. Kids — and adults, for that matter — don't use drugs because some sleazy person in a back alley coerced them into it. Nor do they drink alcohol because they're thirsty and it tastes good. For most teens the taste of alcohol is only bearable, but after a while they get used to it. Then they develop a taste for the high, if not the flavor. The same holds true for other drugs.

Unfortunately, it is easy for drug use to get out of hand, but those who lose control never plan on that happening. No one starts out saying, "I want to be an alcoholic and a drug addict." No one wants to be strung out on speed or dead drunk night after night. But the nature of chemical addictions is such that when people are deep into drugs, they are also deep into denial that they have a problem. That is why it is so important that young people never try drugs at all.

Kids drink and use drugs for several reasons: They've bought the societal message that says drugs are fashionable, and they see their role models — parents, athletes, friends, movie stars — using, so they join the crowd. They want to be accepted by their peers. They are experimenting out of curiosity. Often they are looking for relief from their problems and the high takes away the pain, albeit momentarily.

The high from all drugs — alcohol, cocaine, pot, amphetamines, heroin, or prescription drugs — achieves the same effect: all are mood-altering substances. They are *chemicals* that alter normal, healthy, logical behavior. To understand the abuse of these chemicals, we must look at the way society has become overrun with them and the reasons behind their abuse.

Everywhere you look there are drugs. You see them in commercials, on television, displayed on billboards, and glorified in print. You see drugs used or displayed at the movies, on the street corner, in stores, on your favorite sit-com, and in social situations. Drugs are widely demonstrated, celebrated, bought, sold, discussed, and used. Drugs, in legal or illegal forms, are everywhere.

Drugs are so omnipresent that they have become an accepted part of not only the social scene, but of society at large. Society teaches us that the way to handle problems as well as triumphs is with chemicals.

In the United States liquor is undoubtedly the most popular quick fix. Even the once generic word "drink" has come to mean an alcoholic beverage. We celebrate with champagne and console someone by mixing them a drink. An evening meal may begin with pre-dinner cocktails, followed by wine, and concluded with after-dinner drinks. Parties are rated on the availability of liquor.

Liquor is a social Band-Aid. Feeling a little uptight because you don't know anyone at the party? Have a drink. Feeling a little tense because you do know everyone at the party and you're bored? Have a drink.

It is not only teenagers who bow to peer pressure. Many adults drink not because they want to, but because it is the thing to do. It is comforting to be in a crowded room and to see everyone holding a glass, smiling, and enjoying the occasion.

There are also drugs for ill health as well as drugs for just about every bodily condition under the sun — health-related or not. Walk through a pharmacy and you'll see that there's a drug for every need. We're bombarded with chemicals guaranteed to cure us, to help us lose weight, gain weight, fall asleep, stay awake, and bring fast relief every time our bodies signal us that we're abusing them. And liquor stores and pharmacies sell just the drugs that are legal.

Next illegal drugs enter the picture. Marijuana has become almost as acceptable to use as alcohol. It has been deregulated in many states, sending the implicit message that it is all right to have it and to use it. Yet the sole purpose of marijuana is to make the user feel better or different. When did we lose our internal ability to feel better? We have come to depend on chemicals to stimulate our emotions.

I've heard parents say that they don't understand the disturbance about marijuana. *They* smoked pot when they were young and it had little or no effect on them. What they often don't realize is that drugs have evolved over the last 20 years. Illegal drugs, whether coming in from other countries or being cultured and produced here, are more potent then they used to be. Marijuana grown in Mexico used to have a level of THC (the chemical that produces the high) of about 2 percent. Now, with advanced breeding techniques, the THC level in marijuana is frequently 12 to 18 percent. Once marijuana use begins it often, but not always, leads to experimentation with and then to dependence on more potent drugs.

Other drugs also have become more powerful through new processing and using techniques. It is not enough anymore just to snort cocaine. People smoke it, inject it, and "crack" it. There seems to be no limit to what drug users will do to make the high a little more intense and a little longer.

Illegal drugs are being transported into this country and purchased at record rates because people want them. Cocaine use has hit epidemic proportions. Heroin use remains steady in spite of its certain death sentence. This country is awash in drugs and the effects of drug use.

The drug trade flourishes because the demand is there. Street gangs have become so successful at selling drugs that they export members to other cities to open new markets. Gang members have visibility, they have money, and they have acceptance. That makes using and selling drugs appealing to those who feel their lives are hopeless or to those who want to make a fast buck. And the law-enforcement problems associated with increased drug trade — murders, burglary, and other violent crimes — are multiplying so fast that the police in most cities are overwhelmed and almost helpless to deal with the onslaught.

Drugs are big business. Pot production is the number-one industry in many states. Our neighbors in Central and South America produce many tons of illicit drugs daily. It has been estimated that the U.S. Drug Enforcement Agency, with the help of the Coast Guard, intercepts only about one in 10 shipments coming from the south.

Legal or illegal, drugs have become very much a part of the American scene. They are readily available and they are socially acceptable. It is no wonder that younger and younger children are being "turned on."

Alcohol and Drugs Linked to Depression

Drugs demand a huge emotional price: that is why we are talking about them in a book on teen suicide. Alcohol and many other drugs are depressants, and their use leads to depression. Alcohol, for example, contains ether, an anesthetic used during surgery. It may stimulate one temporarily, but it also acts on the central nervous system as a depressant. Kids looking to forget their pain get the "high," but the lows are lower and come more often.

The end result of drug and alcohol abuse is suffering. The emotional pain that kids experience and the problems that occur because they are drunk or loaded are only one small part of the damage that alcohol and drugs inflict. But these emotional issues, along with the effect of alcohol and many drugs on the nervous system, do cause depression, or deepen an existing depression.

Drugs, including alcohol, are dangerous. They are readily available, and our young people have to deal with them. This brings us to the question: Why do people want to change their moods artificially? What is going on in their homes, jobs, schools, or neighborhoods that makes them want to alter their normal state? Let's look at some of the reasons that kids take drugs.

Why do Kids Take Drugs?

Experimentation

Experimentation is the rationale for the kid who snitches a cigarette from his mom's pack and goes behind the garage to try a puff. Natural curiosity characterizes the young person who takes a little sip of beer to see how it tastes. But simple experimentation doesn't last long.

It is one thing to taste beer once or twice and another thing when the experimentation continues on a regular basis. Experimentation can develop into regular use because kids who experiment quickly learn that it gives them stature and a semblance of maturity that they don't get from being "just a kid." They do it and then brag to their friends that they got drunk on Saturday night. Most likely the boast is a lie. Probably they took a drink, hated the taste, and spit it back out, but they did something only adults are supposed to do, and this elevates their status among their peers. Many kids will continue drinking to hold that admiration.

The next step is to involve friends in the "adventure" so they all have something to talk about. "Try it," they tell their buddies. "It won't hurt to try just once. If you don't like it, you don't have to do it again." This may seem fairly innocent when teens are experimenting with alcohol, but don't forget that bad things can happen when people — teens or adults — get together to get drunk. Fights, risky dares, and car accidents are just a few of those things.

Drug use may begin out of curiosity or because of a search for feelings of excitement or euphoria. Parents have to be aware when young people cross the line between experimentation and regular use. What began as simple curiosity may quickly escalate into drug abuse. And in these days of sophisticated, dangerous drugs, it may take just one "experiment" to end up addicted or dead.

Peer Pressure

Young people want to be accepted, loved, and successful. If they are not maturing internally by developing values and goals, they become susceptible to the influence of other people. They lose sight of themselves and do whatever it takes to fit in. Drinking or doing drugs helps them feel they're part of a wide circle of other users.

The need to belong is important in all aspects of teenagers' lives. What kids are "supposed" to do when it comes to drugs and alcohol is very evident. Whether or not you know it, at your children's schools there are things that "everyone" does. These may be to go to a Saturday-night kegger or to smoke a little pot during half time at the basketball game. Kids know what is considered the norm, and most will do whatever it takes to be accepted.

The peer-pressure aspect of drug abuse is often difficult to battle because teens are so intent on belonging. It takes strong kids to resist everyone else. (Teenagers are also pressured to drink from people other than peers. Often their families expect them to drink. "Heck, I did a little partying when 1 was in high school," says Dad. "It doesn't hurt anything.") Drugs and alcohol are rampant in schools because using them is accepted — even expected — juvenile behavior. Kids live up to expectations.

I ran into the attitude that everyone has to drink when I was in the Navy. In the military, drinking is the hobby of choice. Every Friday night a group of guys I knew would say, "Miller, let's go get drunk." I was a challenge to them because I was the only person they knew who didn't drink.

When these guys asked me why I didn't drink, I'd always ask back, "Why do *you* drink?" They would look at me in complete amazement. No one had ever asked them "why" before. Drinking was expected behavior; it was what life was supposed to be all about.

One buddy answered my question by saying, "I drink because drinking makes me feel good."

My response was, "I already feel good, so why should I drink?" If drinking becomes an issue for your teenagers, ask them *why* they are doing it. The answer may be revealing.

Many teens' mentality about drugs is not much different from that of my Navy buddies. Consider a typical Friday night for a teenager. First they go to the football game. Next comes the party. Kids don't say, "Let's have a beer tonight." They say, "Let's get drunk!" They drink for one purpose: to get wasted. Once under the influence of alcohol or another chemical, they find themselves caught up in it socially and physiologically. The longer they participate, the harder it is to find their way out of the drug habit.

In a school with immature students, drug use gains an inertia of its own. Use is so prevalent that kids feel they are outcasts if they don't participate. The teen who doesn't have a positive self-image has the hardest time resisting friends' exhortations to use drugs.

On a positive note, there finally is a growing trend among teenagers that it is O.K. to say no to drugs and that kids who choose to stay away from alcohol and drugs are all right. Gradually peer support is building for making a choice against drugs.

Learning to face and solve life's problems without the use of drugs helps young people mature, and it will take all the maturity teenagers can muster to deal with the whole array of non-drug-related problems that confronts their generation.

Escape from Life

Another reason adolescents drink or take drugs is to escape personal situations. Sometimes they have family problems and are trying to survive in a poor environment. They don't yet feel enough in control of their lives to change an unpleasant reality. Instead of building resources for support that would enable them to deal with their situation, they too often retreat to the numbness or high that drugs or alcohol can provide. Then they face not only their original problem but also the potential threat of addiction.

Other teens drink or get high to escape the confusing, unsettling feelings of adolescence. For example, most teens question their self-worth at one time or another, but some of them turn to drugs to help cover up those feelings of inadequacy. The payoff is similar to the reward from experimentation. Kids hold a beer at a party or smoke a cigarette or joint to bolster their self-esteem: "Look at me and what I'm doing. What I'm doing is an adult behavior." They want people to admire them for their maturity.

Upbringing has a lot to do with how teens feel about themselves. My friend Dennis did not receive nurturing. Chances are that his parents were chemical abusers who did not have the interest or inclination to care for their children. Dennis, like many kids, decided to relieve his emotional loss with drug use. It was an easy escape chosen to cover the hurt he faced in his daily life.

Ironically, one of the many impairments left by drug or

alcohol abuse is that it fixates one's stage of development. One can become 20 years old but remain mentally and emotionally at the age of 12 if that was when they began drinking or using drugs. Using may seem like adult behavior, but it actually freezes emotional maturation.

Predisposition

Why is it that in a family with four kids, all raised in the same environment, one becomes a drug abuser? The answer may be predisposition. Medical studies show that children of alcoholics have a high likelihood of becoming alcoholics themselves. Even problem drinkers without a recent family history of abuse often have a thread of alcoholism in past generations. Predisposition as a genetic tendency is not perfectly understood, and certainly role modeling is also a factor in families who abuse chemicals.

Predisposition may be the best reason to teach children that drugs and alcohol must be left alone. Some of us may be genetic time bombs who need only to drink or use drugs in order to trigger addiction tendencies. Teenagers should be told that it is better never to know whether or not they have those inclinations than to suffer through the pain and hard work of recovery from abuse.

People use drugs and alcohol for many reasons. (We have discussed only a few.) We must teach kids early that drugs and alcohol are unnecessary and are to be avoided. Here are ways to teach your children about drugs so that substance abuse does not become a part of their lives.

The Solution: Fighting Back

Parents can fight drug abuse by giving young people a clear, definite message about drugs. "You are not to use drugs" is a clear message that can be supported with the ideas listed below. "My kids know better" or "My kids don't do that" are not clear messages. Kids *don't* know better and they *do* "do that" because they haven't been told differently. Every parent must address the issue of drugs and alcohol as early as possible so that adolescents will be armed with accurate information to help them make educated decisions.

"Just Say No"
The "Just Say No" program became well-known because it was supported by a popular presidential administration. "Just Say No" offered a direct, if oversimplified, way for corporations to participate and then to claim that they were doing something about the nation's drug problem.

"Just Say No" is a great way to indoctrinate elementary students about the dangers of drugs. But it's naive to tell junior high and high school kids to "just say no." Adolescents are more sophisticated and need more realistic ways to deal with the many pressures to use drugs.

The issue cannot be ignored until your kids reach junior high. A second-grade girl reported being offered a toke off a joint by a third-grader as they rode home on the bus after school. Parents must prepare younger kids by pointing out the consequences of drug use.

I take every opportunity that comes along to talk to my kids about drugs and alcohol. When we pass a car accident I talk about the percentage of accidents in which alcohol or drugs are involved. When there is a television news story about a drug dealer or a user who overdosed, I help them understand that there is a price to pay for using chemicals. I make them aware that many homeless persons are on the streets because of abuse problems. Finally, I build my children's sense of self by telling them how valuable they are — just the way they are.

Role Modeling
One of the best ways to show teens that drugs and alcohol do not belong in their lives is to refrain from using them in

ours. I have chosen to abstain completely, because I feel anything I do suggests to my kids that it is all right for them to do it, too.

My children are growing up in a society that gives drug and alcohol use a solid base of support. To counter that, I want them to know that chemicals are unnecessary. The benefits of social drinking for me are minuscule compared to the message I want to give my children.

Examine your habits. If you like a glass of wine with dinner or a cold beer on a hot day, be prepared to explain to your children the difference between moderate use and excessive use. This may be harder than you think. If you occasionally smoke pot, ask yourself if the "benefits" are worth it. If we truly want our children to believe that drugs and alcohol have no place in their lives, we must first determine what place they have in our lives.

Arm Teens With Information

Teenagers believe facts and hard evidence. They need straightforward examples and up-to-date information about the human costs of drug and alcohol use. Many adolescents are afraid to ask their parents about drugs; they worry that their parents won't understand or will assume they are using drugs because they are asking questions. They need honesty, openness, and someone who will be nonjudgmental when they ask questions or confess to experimentation. Parents can provide not only the facts on drug use, but also a loving sounding board.

When teens have all the information, they can make a decision about drugs. Here is what kids need to be told about drug and alcohol use:

1. There is a price to be paid for chemical abuse.

We must show teenagers the end result of abuse. How far do you have to look to find a life that has been destroyed by cocaine or alcohol? Not very far. There are an estimated 14 million untreated alcoholics in this country. The lives of countless millions more are being ruined by other drugs.

We have to show kids what eventually happens to people who have turned to drugs. Teens naturally focus on the present. They have to be forced to look beyond that one, small, here-and-now block of time on which they tend to concentrate. They need to see the progression of alcohol and drug abuse.

You don't have to search far to find this progression. Look at Len Bias. He was already a star basketball player in junior high. In high school he was recruited heavily by dozens of colleges. In college his team won basketball's Final Four tournament. He was drafted by the number-one Boston Celtics and signed a contract for $2 million. Three days later he was dead of a cocaine overdose.

When did Len Bias start using drugs? We don't know for certain. He may have started drinking in junior high. He may have done a little marijuana in high school. We do know that his final snort of cocaine was not his first. Drug use was a game to him and he paid heavily. Len Bias was a public figure, but countless John and Jane Does die the same way Bias did.

Drugs and alcohol steal from teenagers, and ultimately teens will realize what they have lost. As Len Bias lived from day to day and triumph to triumph, drugs didn't appear to have a detrimental effect on his life. But he paid the ultimate price: He lost his life for using drugs, and all for what?

Of course the cost of drug abuse is not always one's physical life. Drugs also steal motivation and ambition, and they can maim as well as kill. One television commercial shows a young man talking about his pot smoking habits. He's done it for 10 years, he says, and it hasn't harmed him in the least. He's the same person he always was, he continues, and anyone who says marijuana is harmful doesn't know what they are talking about. Then you hear his mother yelling at him from the next room, "Hey, when are you going to go out and get a job?"

Drugs and alcohol stop maturation at the point at which drug use begins. People who were heavy drinkers in high school tend to be stuck in the same rut eight, 12, and even 15 years later. It is an easy trap to fall into, unless teens ask themselves, "What do I want to be doing 10 years from today? How am I going to get there?" If young people invest their teenage years in drugs and alcohol, they are going to be and get nowhere. They must look beyond the immediate.

Some people, often parents who used drugs 15 or 20 years ago and noticed no harmful effects, believe that publicity about drugs is extreme. They worry that the scare tactics used in some campaigns are overdone. I believe that drug commercials using scare tactics don't even begin to convey how scary drug and alcohol abuse really is. A man I know went through high school without using drugs. Then he went to college in the '60s and heard that LSD "expanded" the mind. I don't know how many times he tried it, but LSD completely blew his mind. Today he still lives at home. He can't hold a job. He can't even hold a conversation.

Drugs exact a price, big or small, every time they are used. The price may be only a hangover, or it may be much worse. A doctor who was the brother of a friend of mine started using drugs as a resident to help him get through the long, grueling nights when he was on call. He went from stimulants to pharmaceutically pure cocaine, and after 12 years he died of a drug overdose. He was an intelligent, educated man, and a wonderful doctor, but that didn't protect him from death.

Emotional scarring is another price that users pay. Terrible things happen when kids are drunk or high that wouldn't occur otherwise, because common sense is put on hold. Consider the kid who drinks for the first, fifth, or hundredth time and then runs his car off the road, killing a friend who is riding in the car with him. How does he feel for the rest of his life as he carries the burden of his actions? Can a couple of beers be worth that amount of emotional pain?

Earlier I recounted the experience of Michelle, a girl who was used sexually at a Halloween party. That night was the first time Michelle drank alcohol. What was the price she paid? The guys who used Michelle must have felt guilty about what they were doing, but they were drinking also and their common sense was gone. Is the feeling one gets from alcohol and drugs worth what happened to Michelle, or to the man who used LSD, or to the doctor who took drugs one or two thousand times over 12 years? Ask your kids how big a price they are willing to pay to use drugs and alcohol, and remind them that the price already being paid is astronomical.

2. Drug and alcohol abuse brings physical and emotional aftereffects.

The physical and emotional changes caused by drug use happen to the users and to the people closest to the users: their families. Explain these physical and emotional consequences to your children. The effects of alcohol and marijuana are similar. As they are the most common drugs used by teenagers, we'll focus on them.

First one experiences a high of euphoria and relaxation. Next follows cognitive dysfunction. One can't reason clearly and has a lower attention span. Memory is impaired, concentration is easily broken, and one has poor perception of one's motor activities. Inhibitions and judgment break down, and one can't make rational decisions. With alcohol, tolerance increases after a while and users find they must increase their consumption to achieve the same high. Blackouts — periods of amnesia that can never be restored — may also occur.

Marijuana smoke damages lung tissue. The heart rate increases and blood pressure goes up. Sex hormones are adversely affected. Many people lose their sex drive and females may quit ovulating. Pot has been linked to infertility problems in both sexes. The immune system breaks down, leaving the user more susceptible to diseases. Moreover, because of marijuana's increased potency many of the long-term effects of the stronger THC (tetrahydrocannabinol) levels are yet to be known.

Longtime users of alcohol or pot get out of touch with their feelings and lose interest and meaning in life. Chronic use also promotes paranoia, mild and chronic depression, and a decrease in social skills. The drug becomes the most important thing in users' lives, and they do not communicate what is happening to them.

They become preoccupied with the chemical, and it starts consuming their lives. They deny that it is harmful; they deny that drugs have anything to do with their problems. The hub of addiction is denial.

Those who live with users also become victims of drug and alcohol abuse. Individuals using drugs do not have quality, intimate relationships. They can't discuss feelings and thoughts, and they become less self-aware. Users feel as if they are losing control. With teenagers, their grades drop and their parents start asking why. They withdraw even further and blame the whole family. The family tries to respond, but often they focus on the symptoms rather than on the cause. Addressing the symptoms avoids the real problem: the drug use. Everyone suffers.

Information about drugs and alcohol, their physical and emotional effects and the price they exact must be given to all young people. The more information provided, the better the chance that teenagers will be able to make healthy, educated decisions.

A Healthy Family Model

Families are families by "accidents" of marriage and birth, yet they are crucial to an individual's development and growth. None of us is perfect, and there is not a family in existence without problems. The following guidelines can help strengthen a family unit as well as each person within the family. Strong individuals are better able to resist social and moral pressures to use drugs and alcohol.

Communication

Promote open communication within the family. If you are there for your kids and teach them responsibility, they will want to be part of the family. Show each other respect and spend quality time together. For example, have meals together, listen to each person tell about their day, and talk about how things are going. Plan family activities that are enjoyable to all. Depending on your children's ages and preferences, this may be difficult, but it helps to build memories.

Positive memories are important because they give kids values, a moral system, and a sense of what behaviors are appropriate and inappropriate. Memories are built by going on outings, participating whenever possible in each other's hobbies and interests, taking photos, and talking about your experiences together. "What did you think of the circus?" "Wasn't that a great basketball game?" Having pictures and memories to reminisce about creates a strong family. (A book including excellent ideas for building family memories and values is *Memory Makers*, by James Covert and Jan Smith [S. Amato Publications].)

Enjoy time together, but don't push each other away during difficult times. The family should be a place where members can admit their mistakes and help each other work through them. Talk openly about sexuality, drugs and alcohol, religion, and any other topic that comes up, and make sure no one with an opposing view feels condemned. One purpose of a family is to promote individuality, not to discourage it. Develop trust by not projecting your thoughts and feelings in a punitive way. Children then will feel safe to share.

Don't be authoritarian. Have a democratic family approach that supports open sharing. Some families hold regular meetings and let members take turns being "president." They plan vacations, talk about problems, and address any issue that children or parents want to discuss. Whatever works to open communication is worth a try.

Use communication skills to work on compromise and flexibility, rather than getting locked in a win/lose power struggle. "You lose, I win," makes individuals feel trapped, and it cuts off communication.

Always show unconditional love. The family should be a refuge of mutual love, understanding, and respect where individuals feel safe no matter what is happening. With so many directions to take and decisions to make as we go through life, it is crucial to have a bonded family unit that can communicate and share those choices.

Priorities

Determine priorities in your family. We live in a materialistic society that equates success with what we have rather than who we are as people. What are our feelings, our memories, and our goals? What do we feel threatens us? What do we feel comfortable with? Make the family priority to explore these ideas instead of to collect possessions.

Safety

It is essential for both parents and teenagers to feel safe. Parents may not feel safe in admitting mistakes, because they are afraid they'll lose respect or authority. Actually, adolescents respect you more when they know that you make mistakes too. Parents need to realize that teens will love and accept them even when they fall short in their own eyes as well as in the eyes of their children. We should all be allowed to make mistakes. To recognize that builds togetherness.

Teenagers need to feel safe and to know that if they try drugs and alcohol, they won't be condemned or rejected by their parents; rather, their parents will show them unconditional love and support so that they can talk through problems and work them out together.

Discipline

Discipline your children starting at an early age, and be consistent. Young people naturally will stretch, push, and pull to test your boundaries. That is where discipline is required. Discipline means that parents love their children enough *not* to move the boundaries back.

We often mistaken discipline for punishment. Discipline, applied constructively, is a way to make young people feel secure because they learn that someone really cares. Always discipline out of love and concern, not anger.

Commitment

Family members share a commitment to each other. If the parents are not committed, their children know it. They feel unloved and are resentful. Their sense of well-being is in jeopardy. Kids often start using drugs to numb those feelings.

This may be a scary thought, but acceptance comes easily in a drug crowd. When children have to change schools, kids who do drugs are the first group willing to welcome them with open arms. They are the least judgmental and the quickest to fraternize with newcomers. A strong family commitment provides students with the support they need to be secure in themselves. Then acceptance doesn't have to come from an outside source.

Recognizing Drug Use

No parent wants to have to look for signs of drug or alcohol abuse. Unfortunately, its prevalence raises concerns for parents of students from the most rural parts of the country to the big cities. Drugs and alcohol are readily available, and our kids know about their availability in grade school and on up. Kids are less naive than their folks. It is better to be armed with knowledge about substance abuse than to live through the consequences unprepared.

Symptoms of Drug and Alcohol Abuse
The following lists of symptoms are not necessarily in order of importance or appearance.

Physical Symptoms
Irregular sleeping habits
Dilation of pupils
Reddening of the eyes
Tremors or shakes
Loss of weight
Dry mouth and excessive drinking of fluids
Unusual tiredness and sleepiness
Unusual energy
Bowel problems
Changes in skin color
Rashes on the skin
Sporadic menstrual periods (for females)
Hair loss and rotting teeth (with severe amphetamine use)

Emotional or Behavioral Symptoms
Irritability — less tolerance for small annoyances
Dissatisfaction
Placing blame on others
Swings in mood from enthusiasm to despair
Loneliness
Isolation from friends
Isolation from family
Communication breakdowns and lack of interest in
    participation in family activities
Changing values — saying and doing things that aren't
    like them, including lying, stealing, and breaking rules
Lack of motivation
Change in homework patterns and grade averages

Denial that anyone can help them
Denial of what they are thinking and feeling
Anger with themselves and others
Fearfulness
Defensiveness
Hints that they don't want to live — the "I don't care"
    attitude of the fourth warning sign

What To Do if You Suspect
Drug or Alcohol Abuse

Check your motives. Why do you want to address this issue? Is it because your teenager is creating a problem or a hindrance in your life? Are you embarrassed by their actions and how others view them? Or is it because you care for your child and truly want to help?

Don't draw conclusions or make judgments. If you are judgmental, defenses will go up and you will push the teen away. Blame cannot be part of the conversation. You have to approach the issue with the motive that you want to know what is happening for the child's sake, not yours.

Remember that substance use may alter their moods. They are not themselves. For example, if you had a colicky baby who cried every evening from four until six o'clock, you accepted that the fussy baby wasn't the sweet little thing you lived with the rest of the day. The baby responded to a physical symptom, and you recognized that response as colic. So, too, does a user respond to the drugs that cause the physical symptoms. Recognize that when your child is on drugs, you see the drug-using characteristics, not your true child speaking to you.

Sit down with your teenagers and tell them the observable symptoms of substance abuse, both physical and verbal. Report behavior and be very specific. As you outline what you have seen, listen to the teen's responses for reasonable explanations or further symptoms of drug use.

"When I asked you to clean the garage, you yelled at me and

said I was asking too much of you. You stomped into your bedroom and locked the door." Do not judge the behaviors. Simply state what was seen. Also report the verbal clues if you inadvertently overheard phone calls or conversations that seemed to indicate that substance abuse was occurring. While reporting your observations, reinforce that you care for them and are doing this because of your love for them.

Next, formulate an agreement to rectify and change the problems. Make a contract to see whether these behaviors will indeed pass or whether they are drug-related. If the problems are drug-related, teens will not be able to hold up their end of the agreement.

The length of the contract should be three or four weeks, with the understanding that if the contract is broken, you will immediately follow through with consequences. If you don't follow through, the teen will lose respect for you. Your lack of follow-through will also reinforce the negative behaviors at issue.

To set up the contract, use these statements: "When you (behave in a particular negative way), I feel (angry, frustrated, sad, hurt, concerned, etc.). I need (appropriate behaviors you want to see)." Issues that might be addressed in the contract include curfew, responsibilities to the family, and school responsibilities such as attending class, showing grade improvement, or doing homework.

Write the contract and have everyone involved sign it. If teens want to "prove" they aren't using drugs, they should be willing to work with you.

If the contract is broken, whether two days later or three weeks and six days later, another meeting should be held. State: "The contract was broken and there has not been an improvement in your behavior." Continue to be nonjudgmental and to report what you have seen. "Joe, you said you'd attend classes, but we just found out that you've missed three classes in the last week. What happened?" Listen to the explanation with an open mind, but be prepared to follow through.

If the negative behaviors persist, the student should be given a drug and alcohol evaluation. Call a treatment facility and ask if they do evaluations and assessments. At most centers there is no charge for these.

The evaluation and assessment is a diagnosis of early, middle, or late stages of chemical dependency using indicators that have been developed for this purpose. A mental and emotional history, a drug and alcohol use history, and a family history are taken. Questions are asked in several ways to determine if there is denial (there almost always is) and the strength of that denial. Following the evaluation, the counselor makes a recommendation that includes a diagnosis and a prognosis of the patient's condition with and without help.

At this point parents often feel a sense of failure and embarrassment. They may want to control the child and make the child quit taking drugs. *But the parents didn't cause the problem, they can't control it, and they can't cure it.* The child needs to face his or her problem and take the responsibility for it, with the parents' support.

Supporting a Chemical Abuser

Every chemical abuser is different. Some users come from single-parent homes; some from extended families. Some are educated, some are not. There is no social, economic, or ethnic discrimination when it comes to drugs and alcohol. But whatever the situation is, the problem can be faced and dealt with through education and a willingness to change. Parents are vital to a chemical abuser's recovery, and parents may also need to make changes in their life and parenting styles. Here are some suggestions.

Develop communication skills. Be open, dependable, and consistent. Let kids tell you how they feel when you are inconsistent. Help them become responsible for what they do by enacting logical positive or negative consequences for good and bad behaviors. Logical consequences help improve judgment.

Plan family activities. Talk to teens when you're hiking, camping, fishing, or bowling. Make it fun to talk and be together.

Let them know you love them unconditionally. Use communicative statements: "I feel . . . " and "I would appreciate . . . ." In a dysfunctional family there are three rules: Don't talk. Don't trust. Don't feel. Reverse these.

As memories from the past reemerge, be honest. Express the situation and how you feel as a result. Talk about the feelings and what caused them. People often have to relive old memories before they can build new ones.

If necessary, give your child permission to use you as a screen for old friends. The parents of one girl I worked with didn't know which of their daughter's friends were users and which weren't. She told her "using" friends that her parents wouldn't let her see them. She wasn't strong enough to tell them she didn't want to see them. She let her parents be the heavies.

Do not expect that after treatment your child will be "fixed" and everything will go back to normal. The child will have the same problems, the same needs, and the same fears, and will be the same person. The difference is just that he or she will not be using drugs.

The old patterns and behaviors may reemerge. This can be the beginning of a relapse, which is not a single event but rather a slow or fast progression back to old habits. Report with love the old behaviors you are seeing. Often users have blind spots and are unaware of what they are doing. Always show love and understanding, or trust diminishes. *Remember, the parent's goal is to understand, not to condemn.*

Support for parents and other family members can be found at Al-Anon, a group for the families of alcoholics and addicts. For a parent who is a child of an alcoholic, ACOA (Adult Children of Alcoholics), is another group that can help. These groups teach such skills as detaching from your child and not getting "sucked into" their problems emotionally. They promote living happily regardless of the child's actions, and they offer constructive ways to handle issues that will come up. They can help you and other family members to heal.

Questions and Answers

1. All kids drink beer once in a while. It's just part of growing up. I did it as a kid. What harm does a little bit of drinking do?

I believe that drugs and alcohol should have no part in our society. People say it's O.K. to drink "a little bit," but how do they know when a little becomes a lot? No one wants to become an alcoholic or drug addict. But it happens. I can't condone drugs and alcohol at all, because I see no use or need for them.

I'm not going to be illogical and say that nobody should ever drink. What I'm talking about is not experimentation in general, but *when* the experimentation happens. If teenagers are depressed, the worse thing they can do is to experiment with drugs and alcohol to help them feel better. It will only intensify the depression they are already feeling. If your kids are experimenting to see what it's like to get drunk, make sure they're not doing it because they are hurting and want to feel better.

2. How much drug and alcohol abuse is normal for a teenager? How do I know when it is too much?

I don't know very many teenagers who haven't tried getting drunk at least once. I would refer a teen to treatment when the abuse starts affecting the child and family in an adverse way. Drunkenness six or more times a year is considered an indication of alcohol misuse. If you see behavioral changes, if your kids are drinking and driving, or if they are having problems at school, something is wrong. Get help for the problem.

3. What can I do to keep my kids off drugs?
Education is the answer. Kids need to be educated about the dangers of drugs. Lots of people will tell them that drugs aren't bad. When I was in high school I heard all the stories too: This is cool. People who say drugs are bad are square. This stuff is great. It won't hurt you. I do it and it doesn't hurt me.

You have to counter this by helping your kids to see where drug abuse leads. Don't be afraid to sit down and talk about alcoholism and drug abuse. For example, if you see someone who is homeless, explain that homelessness is one picture of chemical or alcohol dependency.

Don't let young people think that only the homeless are abusers, because many "functioning" people are abusers, too. If a family member or a friend is an alcoholic, tell your children about the difficulties that the person has experienced because of it. Emphasize that it is not just strangers who have problems with drug and alcohol abuse.

When I read a story in the paper that shows how drugs and alcohol affect people's lives, I point it out to my children. I do this over and over and over. You can't tell them once, "Don't use drugs because they are bad for you," and then consider them drug-proof. The pressure on them to use drugs is monumental. There will be people telling them all the time how great drugs and alcohol are and encouraging their use, so you have to constantly reinforce the true picture of drug use.

4. Are kids drinking and using drugs more than they were a few years ago? Why?
Yes. I think the reasons are that drugs and alcohol are readily available and that there is more pain and pressure in kid's lives.

5. What drugs do kids use the most?
It depends. This question can only be answered by each school or social group. When I go to a school I ask what the

drug of choice is. Sometimes it is pot, sometimes alcohol. Alcohol tends to be the drug of choice in the Pacific Northwest where I live, but every school and community has its own problem.

6. What's the difference between drinking and smoking pot?

Nothing, except that one's legal and the other's illegal. Even though alcohol is a legal drug and is socially acceptable, it isn't any better for you. It is still a drug.

If cocaine came in a liquid form and you could mix it with orange juice or grapefruit juice or tomato juice, and then you gave these cocaine drinks cute names like High Hat, High Ball, or Black Russian, would that make it any less a drug? Does cooking marijuana into brownies make it any less a drug?

Both alcohol and marijuana are chemicals used to alter normal, rational behavior. I see no difference.

7. How can kids get help for friends using drugs?

I often have kids come to me and tell me something like this: "My friend has a major drug problem. He's always high and no one knows. The school doesn't know. His folks don't know. What should I do?"

I ask them why they haven't told somebody. Their response is usually that they're afraid their friend will get mad. I tell them, "Your friend is doing something very harmful that may do permanent damage in their life. A true friend will do something about it, not just watch it happen. A true friend will get them help."

Then I tell them that their friend *will* get mad at them. But even if the user is angry now, a true friend reports the problem because they care and want to help.

A school counselor is a good person for teenagers to tell about friends who have a drug problem. They can also go to clergy, parents, or any adult they trust and continue talking until they find the right person to help.

8. If I know my children's friends are using drugs, should I call those kids' parents? Should I assume my kids are using drugs also?

I would certainly tell the friends' parents because I'd want to be told if my kids were using drugs too. I'd also do whatever I could to help the users. That is the main point behind education for our kids and ourselves. We have to stop looking at "my kid, your kid"; we have to start helping kids, period. We have to attack drug and alcohol abuse where it's happening.

It's easy to say that abuse of drugs and alcohol doesn't affect you because no one in your family uses them. But how many people die every year in motor vehicle accidents because the guy in the other car was using drugs? Substance abuse affects all of us.

Don't assume that your children are using drugs if their friends are doing so, but carefully look at the possibility. When I was in high school my friends used drugs and I didn't. I would not have wanted my parents to assume I was guilty by association. But at the same time, if my children's friends are using drugs, I know there will be a lot of peer pressure on them to participate. I need to be aware when my children are in a precarious situation.

9. My kids have grown up in a loving, stable home. They won't use drugs, will they?

What difference does that make? Anyone who is unaware of the danger and potential harm can be lured into using drugs. Kids from stable as well as broken homes use drugs. Kids whose parents are wealthy as well as kids whose parents are poor use drugs. Don't stereotype. Any child could succumb to drugs.

7

Sexual Abuse

"Be ever gentle with the children God has given you."
— Elihu Burritt

Gresham Union High School

The first person I ever dealt with who'd attempted suicide was a 13-year-old girl I met in a Portland hospital about 1980. I was at the hospital to see Cathy, a friend who'd had surgery, and this 13-year-old was in the bed next to hers.

I asked, "Who's the little girl?"

"That's Rose," Cathy said.

"What's wrong with her?"

"She tried to kill herself."

"Oooh, that's yukky. How did she do it?"

"She took a bottle of sleeping pills and then tried to poison herself by drinking a quart of rubbing alcohol."

"Man, that is disgusting. Why? Why would she do something like that? What was so terribly wrong?"

"I don't know. She won't talk to anybody. She won't talk to the doctors, the nurses, me, or anyone who comes to see her. She won't say a word. She just lies over there, and every once in a while she'll cry."

I kept thinking about Rose. The next time I went to the hospital to see Cathy, the nurse told me Cathy was getting X rays and would be back in about 20 minutes.

When I walked into the room Rose was alone, lying in her bed facing the door. I thought, "Mike, you're real personable. Talk to this little girl." So I went in and said, "Hi, Rose!"

All she did was roll over and face the window. Let me tell you, I'm not a total doorknob, O.K.? I knew this kid wanted to talk to me, but just from a different angle. So I walked around the bed.

"Hi, Rose!"

She rolled back toward the door. "Hi, Rose!"

Back to the window. "Hi, Rose!" She flipped and lay face down in the bed.

What I did next was totally weird for normal people but totally normal for me: I climbed on top of her bed. Now I was standing on the white hospital bed straddling this little girl, looking down at her, in a hospital where I knew almost no one.

I said, "Hi, Rose."

The first thing that Rose said to me, after she rolled over on her back and looked up, was, "You're nuts."

"I'm nuts! You tried to kill yourself. How come? You know you want to tell someone, why not tell me? I'm not a doctor, I'm not a nurse, I won't write anything down on your chart. I don't know who your family is, I don't know what school you go to, and besides, I'm nuts anyway! Talk to me."

She started to cry and said, "You can't help me. Nobody can."

I said, "Hey, you're talking to Mike Miller. I can run into tall buildings in a single bound."

She laughed, and I got down off the bed and asked, "What is wrong, Rose?"

She looked at me and said, "I tried to kill myself because my stepfather's been molesting me, and I would rather die than get pregnant and have his baby."

Let me tell you something. In this country it is estimated that one child out of three will be molested before reaching adulthood. It happens to a lot of people. If it happens to you, you need to talk to someone about it. Deal with it. It doesn't just go away.

Abuse is unfortunate, but it does happen. It is part of our society and it greatly effects our youth in devastating ways. Unlike drug and alcohol abuse, which may be choices kids make, sexual, physical, and mental abuse are imposed on innocent young people who are not given a choice.

Abusers are family members, close friends, classmates, religious leaders, doctors, neighbors, and other adult authority figures in our kids' lives. Abusers are involved in church, scouts, clubs, daycare centers, and sports groups. They are rarely strangers.

Abusers come from all walks of life. They represent every profession, race, education level, and economic stratum. Most appear to lead "normal" lives. For some their inability to cope with the stresses of day-to-day living brings on their abusive behavior. For others deviant sexual behavior began many years before. Many of them were abused as children — although that is not an excuse to abuse others. Very few abusers are unable to control their actions, nor are they "crazy".

No child or adolescent is immune to sexual, physical, or mental abuse. It is difficult to talk about and a subject many people don't want to discuss. But abuse is happening and it's close to our homes — if not in them.

Consider these statistics: In 1986 there were 2,086,000 documented cases of child abuse in the United States. Today approximately one-third of American families experience domestic violence. In at least half of those cases children are involved. Even where children are not the victim, they still suffer from the violence. In 1988 reported child abuse deaths in this country rose 5 percent, totaling 1,225 lost lives. The actual number of children who died because of abuse is probably much higher. Abuse is not only underreported, but it is so common that many social service agencies are unable to deal with the huge load of cases that comes in day after day, week after week, year after year.

There is no doubt that abuse touches us all. A few years ago I spoke at a church luncheon for about 100 women. I asked the women to bow their heads, close their eyes, and raise their hands if they had ever been sexually abused. Two-thirds of them raised their hands. I asked, "How many of you are still feeling hurt over that?" Very few lowered their hands.

I don't think we will ever know the full impact of abuse on the lives around us. Sexual molestation is especially under-reported and, consequently, undertreated. Adults who have been abused often bury the memories and deny the effects of the abuse. They have difficulties in relationships and suffer from chronic depression. Only after they bring the awful experiences back to light are they able to begin the healing process. That is why it is so important that we help people suffering from abuse *now*.

Over and over teens come to me following a *Dare to Live* assembly and say, "You know that story about Rose? I think that's happening to me." I've been to schools where as many as 30 girls out of a class of 200 come and tell me they are being sexually molested. Boys come forward too, although it seems harder for boys to talk about abuse than girls.

For people to say anything at all about abuse is not easy. Sexual molestation is such a big secret that many have great difficulty talking about it. Instead they often become terribly depressed, even on the verge of killing themselves, before they finally break down and tell someone what is wrong. They are terrified they'll get in trouble or someone else will get hurt. These kids are told, and believe, that the fault is theirs. They think they brought the abuse on themselves. Again and again I have to tell them that *no* situation warrants abuse, that nothing they did or didn't do incited abuse. The children are always innocent, even when they don't believe they are.

One reason sexual abuse is so underreported is that sexual abusers make young people promise not to tell: "This is our secret. We will never tell anyone about our special times." Some victims are told that the abuse is a "family secret" which must not be revealed. Others simply don't realize that they are in an unhealthy situation. Often they are threatened with terrible consequences if they report what is being done to them. It is not uncommon for abusers to intimidate children by threatening death to them, their families, or their pets. To the offender there is nothing sacred about a child's trust. They buy silence at a high emotional cost.

Kids who don't speak out suffer the consequences. The reasons they don't tell seem logical from the victim's point of view. For some they don't tell because they don't want to be taken from their families, no matter how terrible the home life. They don't tell because they worry that if the abuse stops, the abuser will simply turn to another victim, such as a younger brother or sister. They don't tell because they fear they won't be believed. They keep the pain inside until, like Rose, they feel their life isn't worth living.

Very rarely will a young person "lie" about abuse, but when they do there are several overpowering reasons. They may lie because it is the only way they can get attention for other problems occurring in their lives. Some children will truthfully report abusive behavior to an outside person and then back down when they are face to face with the abuser, especially when it is their father or stepfather. They know they may have to continue living with this person, and they are scared. And sometimes abused children report a similar or "parallel" experience to test reaction to their story.

But adults must understand that a child who lies about abuse is still a child who is hurting. Whether they have been abused or whether they are lying, they need help. Given that one child in three will be sexually molested before leaving the teen years (and most of those before they even reach adolescence), chances are that when young people report abuse, they are telling the truth.

There are four main categories of abuse: sexual abuse, physical abuse, mental abuse, and neglect. All have devastating effects on the victims' lives. In this chapter I emphasize examples of sexual abuse, how to help, and how abuse relates to depression and suicide.

One reason behind the continued prevalence of sexual abuse, is that it is surrounded by myths that avoid the real issues behind the abuse. By exposing these myths, we can begin the process of breaking down the denial system that accompanies the "secret" of sexual abuse.

Myths and Facts Behind Sexual Abuse

MYTH: *The child is lying or making up stories.*

FACT: Most children do not have the knowledge or sexual vocabulary to make up explicit stories about sexual abuse. Always believe a child when he or she is disclosing something about sexual abuse. To not act, and accuse the child of lying, could be detrimental and even life-threatening, especially if this unheeded disclosure is discovered by the offender.

MYTH: *The child was being seductive.*

FACT: Oftentimes a child molester interprets a child's need for attention, nurturance, and affection as seductive. Child pornography portrays children as sex objects and as provocative. Children do not know how to be overtly seductive unless it has been taught to them by an offender. Oftentimes a child behaving in a seductive manner is a warning sign that the child has been molested. The responsibility to openly address seductive behavior, and not act on it, belongs to the adult and not to the child.

MYTH: *The child likes it.*

FACT: Often the only attention a child gets is when the actual incest is taking place. The child likes the attention, but does not like the sexual manipulation. This often brings with it feelings of confusion about what the differences are between love and sex, which in turn results in guilt.

MYTH: *Mothers usually know about and approve of the incest.*

FACT: 55 percent of the cases reported are reported by the mother. Once reported, often the mothers are confused and as powerless as their children in dealing with the incest. Sometimes the mother has unmet dependency needs, is sexually withdrawn from the husband, or was abused herself and is therefore unable to objectively see what is going on in the home.

MYTH: *The incest offender is an alcoholic or addicted to drugs.*

FACT: Studies show that somewhere between 10 and 33 percent of incest offenders are alcoholics. Little has been found in the relation of incest to drug addiction.

MYTH: *The child is not harmed by incest and it has little, if any negative impact on the victim.*

FACT: Two-thirds of children who have been sexually abused experience immediate emotional disturbance. Long-term results indicate that psychological disturbance is higher among victims than non-victims. This is especially true in the areas of self-mutilating behavior, and dissociative disorders. Medical traumas including genital injury are numerous. Pregnancy and sexually transmitted diseases also occur in incest victims more often than one would like to believe.

MYTH: *The offender is just a sexually frustrated dirty old man.*

FACT: Most offenders and rapists have other sexual outlets. Misusing their power and authority is their way of gaining control over other people. It is impossible for incest to be consensual because of the unequal power structure between the adult and the child.

MYTH: *Incest only occurs in lower socio-economic groups.*

FACT: Offenders are found in all social classes, races, and religions. Their yearly income falls within the national median.

MYTH: *It will only frighten and traumatize children to openly discuss child sexual abuse with them.*

FACT: Sexual assault must be presented as a safety issue. Vague warnings like "Don't take candy from strangers" and "Don't let anyone ever touch you" can often confuse and frighten children. If sexual assault is presented correctly, it should be no more frightening than talking about car safety, how to cross the street, and planning the household fire escape route. We have to train our children, and avoiding the subject can be unforgivable.

The myths and facts can be hard to look at, but they do give us some hopeful insights. Allowing the myths to continue is continuing a lie. Let's not get trapped in the myths. We now know the facts and can take those facts to where they need to be: to our children. ("Myths and Facts" reprinted from *Triumph Over Darkness,* Wendy Wood, M.A. and Leslie Hatton [Beyond Words])

How to Help

We need to stop child abuse that is occurring now, prevent it from happening to others, and know how to deal with it in our own families or those around us. The majority of child sexual abuse occurs before the age of 13. The median age of children who are sexually abused is 11. Therefore, by the time the child reaches adolescence, the sexual abuse has already occurred. First let's look at how to help prevent abuse in younger children, and then how to recognize signs of abuse.

Do Not Raise Children to Be Victims

When parents insist on blind obedience, kids are raised to be abuse victims. In an effort to ensure good behavior, adults condition kids to submit to the person in charge. "You mind" and "Do what adults tell you" are ways of denying young people the option to make choices.

Obedience is necessary, but not without reason and explanation, and not without further instruction that allows children input and recourse if something is wrong. Telling children to "do whatever your elders say" may ensure cooperation. But if the person in charge says, "Let me touch you here," or, "You touch me there," children think that they must obey or get in trouble. Thus we can no longer teach kids to follow adults unquestioningly. We need to protect young people by teaching them that it is all right to say "no." We must help them distinguish between actions and words that are appropriate and inappropriate.

Educate Your Children to Avoid Abuse

Children can be taught how to avoid situations in which abuse may occur. You've probably taught them already not to take gifts from a stranger and not to get into a car with someone they don't know. Now you need to prepare them to trust their feelings and to report to an adult when things are wrong.

I tell my kids that anything anyone does to them that makes them uncomfortable is wrong. No one has any right to intrude on their personal being. It doesn't matter if the person making them uncomfortable is a parent, their grandmother, or their best friend.

Some people oversimplify sexual abuse by telling kids merely not to allow touching of certain parts of their bodies. The problem with those directions is that they fall short. Many sexual activities do not involve the breasts or genital areas. That is why *how* the child feels about an incident of touching is so important.

Kids should be instructed to report to sympathetic adults anything that doesn't make them feel *safe*, *strong*, and *free*. People of all ages should be taught to trust their feelings about what is uncomfortable to them and instructed that if someone touches them or does something that makes them uncomfortable, they need to tell an adult about it. They can confide in their folks, grandparents, aunts, uncles, nurses, doctors, counselors, teachers, or a good friend. It does not matter whom they choose as long as someone is told, and they must keep telling until someone believes them.

Teach kids early about sexual abuse and continue to talk about it throughout adolescence. As they move into their preteen and teenage years, be as frank as you can about what abuse is and why they need to be aware. Speak to adolescents as if they were adults.

Be Mindful of Your Children's Caretakers

Parents should take protective steps to safeguard young people from abuse. Parents are on the go much more than they were even one generation ago. We leave our children with daycare workers, neighbors, friends, babysitters, older brothers and sisters, aunts, uncles, and cousins. To paraphrase a verse in Proverbs: "You are to love many and trust few." I trust very few people with my children. It is often parents' trust that leads kids into situations of abuse. People who are raising children need to be constantly aware of who their children are with, what they say, and how they feel about the people they are with.

Listen to Your Children

Listen to your kids when they report problems. I'm careful about whom I trust my children to, and afterward I ask my kids questions and listen to their report about how things went. A child may have a legitimate reason for not wanting to be left with a babysitter, but one shouldn't overreact. Kids can feel uncomfortable with someone because of a personality clash or any number of other reasons. Whatever their reason, if they feel uncomfortable, find someone else to stay with them. Trust your children's feelings.

By listening to them and agreeing that they do not have to be around people who make them uncomfortable, you tell your children that they are important and that you respect their feelings. Let them know if they have been told not to tell, they need to break that promise. Assure them that no matter what they say, you will not be angry at them. It is hard for kids to talk about abuse, especially when they feel guilty or at fault.

If your child reports abuse to you, and you are disbelieving, ask yourself why. If you'd believe a stranger off the street who told you she was being abused, why won't you believe your own child? Too often we get caught up in the "it-won't-happen-to-me" syndrome and lose track of what is occurring in our own families.

Educating kids to say "no" and to respond to abusive situations if they happen is the primary tool to help. An abuser does not want the activity to come to light. Some people get away with abuse for years because no one tells.

Investigate and Act on Reports of Abuse

You must determine which situations are and aren't abusive. If your daughter tells you her brother grabbed her inappropriately, you must determine whether the action was purposeful or accidental. If your kids go to grandpa's house and he pats them on the bottom every time they walk by, find out if this makes them uncomfortable. Take the following steps before you fling sexual accusations.

Confront the person who is causing the negative feelings. Grandfathers usually pat grandkids out of love. Although he may not be thinking in sexual terms, he does need to be made aware that even innocent pats can make people uncomfortable. Be direct. When your child says that someone's actions make them feel funny, ask that person, "Did you pat Angie on the bottom when she walked by? Do you know that makes her uncomfortable?" By confronting him, you make him aware of the child's feelings. If he pats her again when she goes by, you know that he is aware of her feelings, has chosen to ignore them, and is touching her for reasons other than sensitive affection.

If the questionable behavior continues, make sure your child is not left alone with that person. Your responsibility as a parent is to be certain your kids are not at risk from *any* person at *any* time. If your children say they don't want to go to grandpa's house, there is a valid reason. Young people know whom to stay away from, and their instincts should be trusted.

Sometimes kids aren't very specific about what is going on. A child may say, "My uncle makes me feel funny." The parent can take that statement at face value and not follow through, but the wise parent will ask for specifics. "What does he do that makes you feel funny?" Don't assume that an activity didn't happen if kids don't give you a detailed description of it. Children test the waters first. They see what their parents' reaction is before they extend their trust and become more specific with information.

Kids generally don't make up stories of abuse. Questioning their feelings tells them you are doubting their instincts. Any report of unusual or uncomfortable feelings should be taken seriously. Listen for your children's feelings, not just for their words.

If abuse is occurring, move to resolve the issue. Find counseling, if necessary, remove the child from the situation, or remove the perpetrator from the home to protect the family.

Learn About Child Abuse

Child abuse does exist. Educate yourself. The more you know about abuse, the greater the chance that you will recognize the signs of it. If one or more of the following signs are present, look beyond the behaviors to what the teenager is trying to say.

Signs of Abuse:
Unkempt hair, nails, or clothes
Withdrawal, sadness
Changes in behavior (see the first warning sign for
    depression)
Childishness in behavior or manner for one's age
Precocious knowledge about sex or sexual activities
Physical or emotional self-destructiveness
Covering up or lying about where he or she received
    cuts, bruises, or injuries
Fear of members of a specific sex
Running away
Shoplifting

Overeating and undereating
Refusal to attend gym class, fear of undressing with peers
Struggles with peer relationships
Sleep disturbances and nightmares
Lying, stealing, delinquency
Bed wetting
Detachment — separating their person from their body
Overprotectiveness of siblings
Lack of normal personal contact between offender and abused
    (if, for example, the child avoids their touch)
Overprotectiveness or overattentiveness from the abuser
    toward the child

Reach Out To Others

Reach a helping hand beyond your own family. If your teenager says a friend needs a place to stay, be willing to open your home. Kids in trouble are seeking a safe place. Someday it may be your teen who needs refuge in a friend's house. Here are some ways to offer more than just a bed:

Find out as much as the visitor is willing to tell you about why he or she needs a refuge. Be a good listener. If the person is not willing to open up, just be there.

Often kids in bad situations go to friends' homes to see if the friends live in a loving environment. They are checking to see what a normal family life is like. Children from dysfunctional families don't know that other people live differently. They think happy families are an exception to the rule, because to them the situation they are in seems normal.

If a child takes you into their confidence and tells you about abuse, instruct the child about what can be done to change the situation.

Explain that the law is available to protect them, and tell them what steps will be taken after they report the abuse. If you don't know what occurs when child abuse is reported, call the state or county agency that works with children and families in your area. It is a big step for an abused child to decide to call in the authorities, and they should be supported in this decision.

If you are in a position to do so or if the child wants you to do so, speak to the family. Sometimes families that are confronted admit they have a problem and are willing to work on it. Counseling is available for persons in all economic situations.

Keep Reaching Out

The best way to help is to reach out and to continue reaching out, no matter how many times the individual rejects your help. Just because they don't ask for help doesn't mean they don't need it. Remember, in the later stages of depression — and certainly when abuse is at the core of the depression — young people can't reach out for themselves.

One young woman who was abused as a child and adolescent was finally removed from the abuse when she was 17. She moved into foster care, but because of her previous history she was unable to believe that her foster parents could love her. It took 12 years for her to come to know that they loved her for just being herself. Keep reaching out to those you suspect are being abused — even if it takes them 12 years or longer to know you really care and want to help.

Report Abuse to the Authorities

When you suspect abuse, call the authorities. This is a hard step to take, but if you believe that someone in your neighborhood or circle of acquaintances is being abused, get involved.

Become aware of what is happening around you. If the neighbors' children are outside in all kinds of weather, if they can't get into the house because the door is locked, if they always seem to be hanging around your house at dinner time hoping for a meal, there is a problem.

At this point you need to decide how you can do the child the most good. Kids who grow up in an environment of abuse or neglect develop a sense of low self-esteem and self-worth. That is how depression begins.

Try talking to the mother or father first to see whether the situation can be corrected. Often people who physically abuse or neglect children do so because they feel they have no other options. You may be able to help them explore possibilities they hadn't considered: "If your kids need a place to stay while you're at work, let's make arrangements," or, "If you are frustrated and feel like hitting your son, call me and I'll watch him while you go for a walk."

It is hard to confront a friend, neighbor, or acquaintance, but more people must become willing to step in. Ask yourself if the abusive actions or words were being used against you, would you like it? How would you feel in the child's position? Whether to confront the parents or not is a personal matter, but be as brave as you can for the benefit of the children.

If nothing changes after you've talked to the parents, report the situation to the authorities.

Stop Abusive Behavior and Seek Help

If you are a child abuser, stop the abuse *now*. Seek help for yourself and your family. Talk about it. If you're not sure what kinds of behavior are abusive, consider this definition: Child abuse occurs when someone cannot or will not control his or her physical or verbal anger or sexual behaviors toward someone else. Neglect takes place when an authority figure withholds or cannot provide food, shelter, and clothing for a dependent.

Abuse and Depression

Child abuse — sexual, emotional, physical — causes depression. I worked with one young man, a "B" student, who was living in his car in the parking lot of the high school. He told me that he didn't know where his mother was; she had run off when he was four or five. His father had remarried, and he didn't get along with his stepmother.

A few weeks earlier the boy's stepmother had given his father a choice: either the teenager went or she did. The father ran a trucking business, and his wife was his bookkeeper. He told his son, "I'm sorry, you're going to have to go, because she does the books and I can't run the business without her." This boy was wondering if he had any reason to live.

Abuse, suicide, and depression are closely related because children who are abused have poor self-images. They don't like themselves, they don't feel valued by others, and they don't like what the world has given them. They don't like the fact that they've grown up hungry for love and having to ask for help. It isolates them and makes them different. They feel an emptiness that can't be filled, and often feel deprived, unloved, and abandoned.

Abused children believe that love is conditional. They don't know that love need not involve having to give sexual favors or being smacked around. They don't realize that love can be given freely — with no strings attached. Without this kind of love they place little value on themselves or their lives. It is virtually impossible to escape depression when you are trapped in a situation you know is wrong with a person you might love and yet hate, but are without the maturity to know how to make it all stop.

Abused children feel no hope, and it often seems to them that no one cares. They look for love in all the wrong places; they don't know where the right places are. They try to escape the situation in any way they can: drugs, alcohol, prostitution, or crime. Some even kill themselves. Suicide, the final act of desperation, is another escape from the pit that is their life.

This is an account written by a 34-year-old woman who had been sexually and physically abused:

"When I began writing my manuscript, I didn't realize I had been suicidal at 17. I didn't realize that because of the way I had been treated by others, I had a poor self-image and didn't like myself.

"I used to pray to God: Why can't I just die? Wouldn't it be easier if I just died and went to heaven, and I didn't have to have this hurt and pain? Even at 12 I was asking God why I had to hurt so much. If there is a God and He really loved me, why did I have to endure this?

"I didn't know I was suicidal at 17 until I sat down and started putting words on paper years later. Then tears started streaming down my face and I couldn't see the paper because of all the pain that was finally coming out. I know now that I was suicidal from the time I was 17 until I was 23 or 24.

"The only reason I didn't kill myself was that I was afraid of the pain. I didn't like the pain of a razor slitting my wrists. I didn't have the guts to take a gun and blow my brains out. If I jumped off a bridge I'd probably have broken my legs. If I took pills — if I had been able to get them — someone would probably have found me before I'd finished the job, and I'd have to get my stomach pumped. Then I'd live anyway to endure more abuse. But I thought through all the possibilities.

"It was easier for me not to commit suicide, and I decided to live with the pain. But I still tried to kill myself indirectly. I betrayed my values over and over for the next 16 years. I didn't think I was pretty; I didn't think I had value. I had been married and divorced; I had three kids; and I had done all the things that I swore I'd never do. I did things that were pure suicide. All because I didn't have self-worth."

A lot of kids are going through a lot of depression because of abuse. People who have been molested must get help to deal with the problems that get left behind long after the abuse stops. Not only have their bodies been used, but their trust has been abused as well. Once they understand that they were victims, they can be survivors.

There are more than two million incidents of child abuse per year in this country alone, and chances are that this number is a gross underestimation. Take the time to find out more about the issues and how you can help. Listen to your children and their friends. Remind teens that they are safe, strong, and free, and to report when they feel otherwise. While these are not "cures" for child abuse, they are tangible things we can do to help.

Questions and Answers

1. What if my child reveals an abusive situation that happened a long time ago?
Deal with it immediately. First, talk to them about it. Next, get them a trained counselor, who will help them understand that they were a victim. Many teens think that if something bad happened to them, it means they are bad. A professional counselor, psychiatrist, or psychologist can help them get over these feelings and proceed with their lives.

Also find out if there is legal recourse, because the abuser probably has been, or is, abusing another youth. Abusers need to be stopped for the protection of all children.

2. How do I know whether or not my child is telling the truth?
If teens claim they are being sexually molested, take it as truth or a parallel reality. I am on their side and act as their advocate. Some kids do exaggerate, but if by some chance they are "lying", how badly must they be hurting to tell a lie that big to get attention? Something is wrong. Either way the child needs help.

3. What happens to a young person who reveals abuse?
Lots of people ask me this question when they tell me about abuse. First the authorities will be brought in, because the

school has a legal obligation to report abuse. Usually the teen is talked to and an investigation begins. If the abuser lives with the teen, an immediate step is made to protect the teen from their abuser. The abuser is charged, and sometimes there is a trial. This process is not easy, and the procedures vary from situation to situation.

If a young person who is being sexually molested wants to find out what will happen *before* actually reporting it, they can pose the problem hypothetically to a school counselor, member of the clergy, youth worker, or authority: "What if this were happening . . . ?" The adult can explain what the steps will be, and the teen can understand the procedure and have their questions answered without the adult being obligated to report the situation, as the situation is only hypothetical.

When children or teenagers are being sexually molested, it must be stopped. They *must* report it — not only for their sake, but for the sake of other children who are or will be the abuser's victims.

4. Why are more girls abused than boys?

More girls report abuse than boys, but we don't know that more girls are abused than boys. 97 percent of abusers are male, but this does not determine their gender preference for victims. Because of social stigmas around boys talking about abuse, there are often fewer male disclosures.

5. What if I was abused as a child? Do I need to bring up all those bad memories?

Yes, you must. I have talked to countless adults who were sexually abused as children, and it has caused them all kinds of problems in their adult lives. Pretending that the molestation didn't happen, or ignoring it, doesn't make it go away. If you have an emotional hurt, you have to deal with the issue, preferably with a trained professional who can help you through it.

8

Love and Respect

"Love is gained freely. Respect is earned."
—Michael Miller

I have come to the conclusion that everyone, kids and adults alike, want two simple things out of life: love and respect. This doesn't seem like a big request, but take away one or both and people become unhappy and hurting.

Love and respect figure in our lives from the minute we enter this world. Let's start with a newborn. No matter how cute a little baby is to its adoring parents, it is basically a lump. Look at that lump when it is a few days old and you know that in just a few years this tiny human will be walking, talking, hopping, and singing. Nearly everything a child does and becomes in that time will be *learned* behavior. To learn these skills requires teaching. In the case of the transformation from lump to person, the teachers are the newborn's parents.

Why do adults take the time to teach little babies? Because they love them. What is the first thing they teach their infants? Love.

Love is the voluntary giving of one's emotions and care to another. A baby is not able to return its parents' love with hugs and kisses, but that doesn't stop the parents from pouring it on. In a short while the baby begins to notice. A funny smile, a way of snuggling in against your neck, or a soft sound tell parents that the developing person inside the little body understands love and is beginning to return it. These early responses make parents do even more to get that goofy grin. The baby responds and the cycle of love is born. This pattern of love and loving responses takes the parents and baby only so far—to about the first birthday, in my experience. Then, obedience must be introduced.

Toddlers have to learn basic obedience and how to respond to parents' directions, even if they don't cognitively understand why. Trying to explain to an 18-month-old about electricity, so the toddler won't stick its fingers into the sockets, is hopeless. Teaching them that a stern "no" means "stop!" is the beginning of obedience training.

But be careful. By the time a child is five or six years old, blind obedience no longer works. From this point on, children need to be told *why* they are being asked to do something. As discussed in the chapter on abuse, insisting on blind obedience from older children sets them up for problems.

"Always do what adults tell you."

"You are a kid. You don't need to know 'why.' "

"Why? Because I said so." The message is to obey without question. Many innocent young people have done so and then have been abused by people who take advantage of their belief that all adults are to be trusted.

If you explain to children why they should obey their parents, you protect them and also introduce the concept of respect. Parents' explanations show that they respect their children as individuals enough to explain why they need their obedience. The Fifth Commandment in the Old Testament of the Bible does not say "*Obey* your father and mother." Rather, it says, "*Honor* your mother and father." Honor is defined as high regard, otherwise known as respect. Parents who teach obedience without the foundation of love and respect for children don't receive back love, respect, *or* obedience.

A parallel of parent-child respect and obedience occurs at the national level. We love and respect the country we live in, and the laws of the land are obeyed because we understand their purposes. This lawful obedience stems from respect, just as children's obedience grows out of the respect they are shown when parents explain their actions or requests to their children. But during the Vietnam War, respect for the United States plummeted because many of the country's "children," or citizens, disagreed with the government's actions. Many laws were ignored or defied. As happened with draft resistance and demonstrations during the Vietnam era, a child who does not respect his parents will not be obedient. And just like love, respect is reciprocal. Once you respect children, they will respect you.

Parents of teenagers want love and respect from their children, but they often neglect to tell that to teens. These "big" kids figure that all mom and dad want is obedience. The magic formula is that love and respect lead to obedience. When young people are taught what is expected of them, when they are loved and respected, obedience will follow.

Giving love and respect to one's children and receiving it in return is an experience that should be instilled each step of the way as children mature. Yet as kids mature they have changing needs. It is difficult to keep up with all they are experiencing and learning. That is why it is all right to tell your pre-teen or teenager, "I've never raised a 12-year-old (or 16- or 18-year-old) before, and I'm not sure how to do it. If I'm doing it wrong, you need to tell me."

Love and respect is a two-way street. We want to teach our children to love and respect us, but we also must love and respect our children. To show love and respect for my kids, I change my parenting style as my youngsters grow and mature. My oldest daughter knows I love to tease. As she grows up I find that there are more and more areas that are off-limits to my teasing. I have told her to tell me when I hit one of her sensitive spots, and she does. When I get too personal, she says, "Dad, don't tease me about that. O.K.?" I *respect* that request. I know that I'm giving her all the love I can, but that I can give her more respect. In this case respect means listening to her special requests and changing our relationship as she grows.

Besides being insensitive to their needs, there are other ways parents can show disrespect for their children. All parents struggle to balance their personal needs with their children's needs. But parents who push young people away out of tiredness, impatience, or boredom are disrespectful of the person they brought into the world. For example, one thing I like to do in the evening is watch the game show "Jeopardy" on television. The show is fast-paced, and I really get into the questions and answers. One night I was absorbed in the show when one of my daughters came in to tell me about something that had happened to her that day. My response was less than perfect: "Can't you see I'm watching 'Jeopardy'!"

She looked devastated. "I just wanted to talk to you," she said as she turned to leave.

I shut off the television and called her back: "I'm sorry. What did you want to tell me?" She is more important than a television program that doesn't matter 20 minutes after it's over! She is my child and I have only one chance to raise her. We must make our kids feel special, loved, and respected.

I am not saying that kids should have your immediate attention whenever they demand it. Instead of snapping at my daughter, I could have taken her hand and said, "Wait just a few minutes until my show is over. Then I can give you my full attention." That would have taught her respect for my needs as well.

My goal in raising my four children is that when they are in their twenties and thirties and are beyond my influence, they will say that I am one of the people in this world whom they respect the most. But for them to say that when they are 25 years old, I have to be available to them at four years old, 10 years old, and 17 years old.

Let's divide the subject of love and respect into two parts: First, what kids need to learn from parents in order to get and give love and respect, and second, what parents need to remember about being a child and an adolescent.

What Teens Need to Learn from Parents

Teens Need to Know What is Expected of Them

Parents gain respect by bringing young people into the family decision-making process. That teaches kids what is expected of them. Explaining our decisions doesn't mean we always have to say "yes," but a "no" answer should include reasons that teenagers can understand. It is not disrespectful for parents to say "no", but *is* disrespectful to say no without an explanation.

Why should you have to explain your actions and decisions to kids? There are several reasons. The first reason is that the ways of a parent can be mysterious to a young person. Adults who pass down orders without any apparent reason seem all-knowing. That makes kids think that mom and dad are omnipotent; in other words, parents don't make mistakes. Although it may seem amusing to be "perfect" to your children, this leads to problems. It is better to admit fault and mistakes, and to explain why you do what you do. To do so gives kids room to fail; it permits your children to be as human as you are.

When parents seem infallible, young people think they are expected to be perfect, too. Yet they feel they cannot live up to their parents' image. To be perfect is impossible, as we all know, and many immature teenagers go hard and fast in the opposite direction to prove that they are only human. Remember the story of Susan in Chapter 2? She knew she could never live up to the image of the "perfect child" in which her father believed, so she quit trying. In fact, she acted up in an effort to prove to her father that she was anything but perfect.

The second reason is that it keeps you from being hypocritical—or it exposes your hypocrisy for what it is. Many of us tell our kids one thing and then turn around and do another. Parents are not perfect, but sometimes they act as if they expect their kids to be. "Don't do what I do," you tell them, "Do what I say." Children receive the double messages this way.

"Eat your vegetables. They'll make you healthy and strong," dad says while he smokes a cigarette.

"Respect me because I'm your father and I deserve your respect," dad says, and then he turns around and belittles mom.

"Tell me the truth! Don't try to hide it from me; I'm your mother." But when mom overcharges at the mall, her instructions to the kids are, "Don't tell your father."

Kids learn from example. Monkey see, monkey do. What goes in comes out. Or, in computer language, GIGO—Garbage In Garbage Out. Young people imitate what they see, not what they hear. There is a saying, "You reap what you sow." Many parents seem to be praying for crop failure. But on the positive side, love still begets love, respect begets respect. If you love and respect your children, they'll see it and imitate it.

In addition to understanding *why* they must be obedient, I firmly believe children should be informed of their "jobs"—the tasks that help them understand and grow into adulthood. What are children's jobs? I consider three things to be of utmost importance for all young people to learn and do.

First, they must learn respect for their belongings. One big problem all parents have is to convince their kids to pick up their possessions. At one time my two youngest daughters had what may have been the world's largest collection of "My Little Ponies" and they loved to scatter them everywhere. If a friend came over to visit, the girls would be gone in a flash. In my experience plastic ponies don't put themselves away. So, I'd call the girls back and calmly state that apparently they no longer wanted their toys, and if they didn't want them, I'd get rid of them. Those two little girls rarely moved faster than that. Just like everything else, respect for belongings has to be taught.

Second, I tell my kids that while I am supporting them, their job is to attend school and to learn. Education is the gateway to the future, and children must understand this.

Third, in every household children should also perform chores or errands that are their responsibilities toward the household maintenance. Even the littlest children can set the table, dust the furniture, or sweep the porch.

These three things—caring for their belongings, attending school, and completing family responsibilities—are roles kids need to learn are expected of them, and they must be told so. Understand that young people know nothing automatically.

Explaining why we make decisions and hand down orders helps children understand adult reasoning and have an accurate picture of the strengths and weaknesses of their parents, and it keeps parents from slipping into hypocritical statements and actions. Telling kids what you expect them to do keeps communication open and teaches them that everyone has something to give and to receive by being a part of the family.

Teens Need to Know Their Boundaries

When young people misbehave, they must understand that there is a consequence to their actions. They need to know the boundaries and consequences that surround them. Compare raising a child to putting a plant in a pot. As the plant grows, the roots expand until they fill the pot. Then the gardener-parent transplants the growing plant into a new, slightly larger pot. Children will test the boundaries of their "pots," but they should not be "repotted" to receive new privileges until they have matured enough to accept the additional responsibilities the privileges bring.

Boundaries are only boundaries if they hold up under pressure. It is up to parents to enforce the boundaries consistently. Consider one family who came to me for help. The daughter, Laura, who was in the tenth grade, was skipping classes at school. The week before she had missed seven classes, and her parents were not making any progress explaining their concerns to her.

I discussed with Laura's parents what consequences she might face for skipping. They decided what action they would take, and they told her, "This is the rule from now on. You will be grounded one day for each class you miss."

The next week Laura skipped class 30 times! She rebelled and did not go to her classes at all. (She did go to school. She just chose to eliminate the classroom part.) At the end of the week when her parents found out, they came back to me and asked, "What do we do?"

I reminded them of the consequence—the boundary—they had set up. But in retrospect they were afraid it was too harsh. So instead of grounding Laura for 30 days—that would have been punishment for her parents too!—they backed off and grounded her for two days.

The first night they took her to a movie because they felt sorry for her. The second night she complained so much that they let her go out with her boyfriend. Why were they so inconsistent? They told me that they liked her new boyfriend and were afraid that if she weren't allowed to go out with him for a month she would lose him. Needless to say, nothing was learned by Laura or her parents.

Boundaries will be broken, which means parents will have to follow through with consequences. But regardless of the consequence or punishment—and there are a variety of choices depending on styles of parenting and kids' personalities and ages—discipline for children must *always* be given in love. Teenagers will push parents as far as they will go. Parents have to push back with love, respect, and explanations that teach kids respect for themselves and their folks.

When you discipline a child or teen, deal with the problem, explain the reason for the punishment, and then *forgive them.* There is nothing worse than being corrected and then having the wrong thrown back in your face. Many kids have told me that their parents do not forgive them for mistakes. Past incidents are rehashed time after time. Consequently, they feel that there is no forgiveness, there is no reason to change their actions, and they continue to do wrong.

It is an emotional beating to have to live down indiscretions that occurred months and years before. Do not keep a running record of wrongs committed. Discipline, correct, and let kids' mistakes go.

(Attention, teenagers: This goes both ways. You have to forgive your parents if they have made mistakes. When my good friends' daughter Alison was in seventh grade, she was looking forward to her first school dance. Without consulting her, her parents volunteered to chaperone. Alison was furious and refused to go to the party. She sat at home while her parents attended *her* first dance. Years later when they were struggling with other teenager-parent issues and problems, Alison was still bringing up this incident. Even when it is hard to do so, there has to be a point at which you forgive.)

Forgiveness is essential, but the common courtesy of saying "I'm sorry" is often abused when mistakes are made. Many times teens use "I'm sorry" to get out of a situation and smooth it over, instead of learning about boundaries and consequences to actions. Apologizing can be a convenient strategy to cover up anger without resolving the problems that caused the anger in the first place.

When one apologizes to one of my friends for a wrongdoing, she asks, "What are you sorry *for?*" What she is asking is, "Do you *understand* why I'm upset?" When parents make sure that kids know what they are apologizing for (instead of just saying "sorry" to get out of the hot water they're stewing in), parents teach them to understand grown-up reasoning. Ultimately, you are teaching them how to function in an adult world.

After receiving your forgiveness, teens must be allowed to prove they can be trusted to act correctly. Trust can be hard to give, but everyone deserves the opportunity to start over. Children live up to parents' expectations. If you expect your child to be a bum, more than likely a bum he'll be. Expect, instead, that a teenager's next opportunity to prove trustworthiness will be successful.

Kids have to know their boundaries and the outcomes when they go beyond those lines. Parents have to enforce the boundaries with consistent consequences and discipline given lovingly, not angrily. Forgiveness for mistakes, by both parents and children, is essential if trust is to be rebuilt. Everyone deserves a second, third, and even fourth chance. After all, we are all human.

Teens Need to Know About Morality and Character

Parents must teach their children morals and character. The most direct way to do this is to model the behavior you'd like to see in your kids. How do you want your children to be? If you want teenagers who are honest and trustworthy, act that way yourself. If you want them to value friends, value yours. If you want them to be kind to others, be thoughtful and caring yourself. This is a simple idea, but it involves looking at your own values and how you pass them on.

While you're at it, don't forget to model love and respect for your spouse. If parents love and respect one another and verbalize it ("I appreciate what you do to support us, honey," or, "I was wrong and I'm sorry"), it will be a permanent lesson for their kids.

Take time to talk about why there are "rights" and "wrongs" in this world. There are endless examples you can use in the daily news or in stories about school that students bring home each day. For example, ask kids why they think it is wrong to take someone's coat and how they would feel if they were the person stealing the coat or the person whose jacket was stolen. Empathizing is a valuable way to teach morality.

Character is a little more ambiguous, but it involves doing the right thing even when it is the hardest thing to do. It can be as simple as giving back the extra dollar you were mistakenly given in change at the grocery store or as hard as passing up a day off to help out a co-worker. Character is subtle, but children who see it modeled will retain those lessons all their lives.

Warning: Immoralities and lack of character can be modeled and taught as well. I grew up in Detroit, Michigan, during the 1960s, when racial tension was high. My parents drummed into my head that people were not to be judged according to the color of their skin. I know now that prejudice is a learned trait. There is no such thing as "natural" bias. Look at two-year-olds who have not yet "learned" about skin color. They will play with any child with no concern about ethnic, religious, or economic heritage. 15-year-olds, however, have had time to learn the differences—*if* that is what they have been taught.

Teens Need to Know How Parents Think and Feel

Young people need to learn about the roles and pressures of being a parent and an adult, just as a parent should try to understand how it feels to be a child or adolescent. It is healthy for kids to know about the problems of your job and the frustrations of making ends meet. Tell your kids how you feel when you get a raise, lose an important client, spend all day cleaning only to find the house a mess two hours later, get angry at a friend, or finish a big project.

Many parents, especially fathers, think that kids should know all this stuff: Kids should *know* they are loved because, after all, dad and mom are working to support the family. But kids don't understand it that way. They are not mature enough to figure it out. Explain to them: "I love you so much that I go to work. I want to stay home with you or be here after school, but I do this for you and us." Kids then know that mom and/or dad work because they love them. They say to themselves, "I'm important. My parents want to provide for me."

Good communicative statements are descriptions of actions and feelings. "When (something) happens, I feel (sad, happy, frustrated, angry). Share your feelings with your children and they will share theirs with you. You will build mutual respect for each other, and your children will gain a realistic view of the world and of parenthood.

Teens Need to Know How
Parents Come to a Decision

Parents make decisions from a mature, adult perspective — most of the time. That means that they reach decisions by considering the problem logically. They weigh the pros and cons, consider the options, and then decide. When you go through this process and reach a decision, share the decision *and* the process with your children. In this way, you provide a model for them on how to make the important decisions they will face as teenagers and young adults.

Teens Need to Know That They Are Loved

I cannot stress this point enough. There is simply no way a parent can tell a child too much that they are loved. If you don't already say "I love you" at least once a day, start now. If you haven't shown your children love, if they haven't felt they are important in your life, it is not too late to begin. Even if you have a 14-, 16-, or 19-year-old, say, "Hey, listen, I've made

mistakes. But I love you." There is always time to start showing love and respect.

In addition to verbal reassurances you can snuggle, pat them
on the back, wrestle with them, hold their hand, write them
silly notes, cheer for them at games, tell them you like them,
tickle them, kiss them, and give them lots of hugs. One study
showed that the optimum number of hugs to keep a person feeling great and functioning well is 12 per day. Most of us are
terribly undernourished when it comes to hugs.

What Parents Need to Remember
About Being a Teen

Gresham Union High School

*I'm a firm believer that when girls turn 12 their mothers take them
to a special school to teach them how to break up with a boyfriend.
The reason I believe this is that girls, nationwide, break up with their
boyfriends in exactly the same manner.*

*This is what happens: Monday morning, our couple shows up at
school, girlfriend looks at boyfriend and says, "We need to talk."*

Guy looks at girlfriend and says, "O.K."

*She takes him over to the corner by themselves and gets this
sorrowful look on her face as if she's seen too many "Little House on
the Prairie" episodes, and she says, "It's over."*

The guy says, "No, school's just starting."

*The girl lets a little tear run down her face, and she says, "No,
the feeling . . . it's gone."*

*Then the guy, suddenly realizing he's being dumped, begs, "No,
please don't break up with me. I love you! I care! You're the only
one I can ever love!"*

*Now not only does the girl have to rip his heart out by the aorta,
but she has to stomp on it. She says that line which we've all heard,*

*every male from Adam on down. She stares him right in the face
and says, "We can still be friends."*

Parents Need to Remember That Being
a Teenager Is Not Easy

Parents have a hard time remembering what it is like to be
between childhood and adulthood. They tend to think their own
experiences should be the rule of thumb for today's teenagers,
even though at least 15 years have passed since their own teen
years. On top of that, almost all of us remember the good times
when we were adolescents, not the bad.

Many kids do not talk to their parents because, even though
the parents mean well, they have a preconceived idea of what
being a teen is all about. These ideas are outdated. The thing I
hear most frequently from the kids I talk to is that their parents
don't understand them. I ask, "Do you understand your parents?" and the teens say "No." *It is the responsibility of parents
to bridge the gap between parents and children, because a
child is only a child.*

Parents, let's look at how different being a teen is now from
when you were one. The world has changed in the last few
decades, extremely in some ways, radically in others. As a
teenager you did not worry about AIDS and herpes. You probably didn't think much about the possibility of a nuclear holo-
caust. The media, with its modern technology, makes ours a
global society. We know about famines, diseases, economic
depressions, ecological disasters, wars, riots, and political unrest all over the world, and within hours of their occurrence.
These pressures alone make growing up more stressful than
when you did it or when your parents did it.

Having busy parents also makes the teenage years more
difficult than before. This is the first generation of children to
grow up at a time when in the majority of families both parents

work outside the home. That has become the social norm, because working parents are an economic necessity in many families and an emotional necessity in others. When parents are busy they have to work twice as hard at making kids feel loved and understood.

I know that the parents of teenagers who feel misunderstood love their kids. I know that their children are of utmost importance to them, and most would be hurt to find out their teens don't feel understood. Often parents haven't taken time to express love or to really listen to their children. These kids are uncertain how their parents feel about them, and if children do not know that they are loved, everything else their parents do is useless. The solution is to tell your child repeatedly that he or she is loved.

Finally, busy parents tend to forget that kids' problems are as real as adults' problems. From our "mature" perspective we tend to minimize what teens are going through. We forget that these problems are monumental to the person experiencing them, no matter how small they seem to us. Don't belittle your child's difficulties, because that only tells a young person to avoid their parents when they have a problem.

When Heidi, my oldest daughter, was in first grade, I went to school to have lunch with her. A little red-haired boy was sitting across the table from us, and Heidi looked uncomfortable.

"Is something wrong?" I asked.

She motioned for me to lean down, and she whispered, "Blaine kissed me."

I asked, "Who's Blaine?" She pointed across the table at the red-haired boy.

"Do you want me to talk to him about it?" I asked.

Heidi nodded.

"Blaine, did you kiss my daughter?"

"No, sir!"

Heidi shot up and yelled, "You liar!"

It was all I could do to keep from laughing, but I looked at Blaine sternly, and he confessed, "I tried. But she turned her head."

Looking as serious as I could under the circumstances, I said, "Don't try anymore."

To my six-year-old daughter that kiss shook her world. It seemed funny to me, but I had to be sensitive to her six-year-old problems if I wanted her to come to me with her 16-year-old problems. I had to try to understand how she felt at that point in her maturity.

Anything that concerns your children is important enough to talk about and deal with, because it tells them that they are important to you. If you don't listen, the message they hear is that their problems are not big enough for you to consider. Then when they *do* face a big problem on which you would like to have input, they remember all the times you rejected their other problems as inconsequential. They'll say, "My folks have never cared about my problems before. Why should they care now?"

The attitude of parents and of any adult who talks to kids should be: "I'll listen to your problems about hair-pulling in first grade and nasty words in second grade so that in seventh grade, when the belief around school is that being a virgin is square, you'll feel free to share that concern with me too."

It is difficult for adults to keep a teenage perspective fresh in our minds. We are often busy with our own concerns and problems, but it is crucial, especially during our children's adolescence, to be understanding about what they are experiencing. You know that you love your kids, but somewhere along the line you may have lost touch with them. This situation can be fixed. Make your children your priority, ask them how they are feeling, and really listen to their responses and problems. With a little time and effort on your part, they will begin to see that you really *do* understand and care.

Parents Need to Know How a Child Comes to a Decision

There are four ways kids reach decisions: logically, emotionally, because of peer pressure, and a combination of these three. When children are young, they are not capable of making a truly logical decision; almost everything is based on feelings. A two-year-old works on pure emotion: "I want that toy because it is pretty, and I want it *now!*"

As children mature they begin adding a little logic into the decision-making process. Ten-year-olds who want to stay up late to watch a movie on a school night will work hard on coming up with "adult" reasons why they should be allowed to do so. The reasons will probably be a mix of logic and emotion. "I promise that I won't be crabby in the morning. I've finished all my homework, and I even helped with the dishes. Please, I just have to see the movie or I'll die!"

When they become adolescents and the need to be accepted becomes paramount, peer pressure becomes an overriding factor. Teenagers can't wear ankle socks, carry a backpack, or bring a sack lunch. There really isn't any reason, except that those things just aren't acceptable behavior. (But watch out. Next year the "rules" will change.)

About the time parents despair, young people mature. It is that gradual maturation, aided by parents, that teaches kids about good, logical decision making.

Let's look at how teens' decision making is likely to evolve. The most common mistake of immature teenagers is trying to make decisions using only one method. Peer pressure is probably the most "normal" yet least desirable way to come to a decision. "Why did you shoplift? Why did you get drunk on Friday night? Why do you have to buy *those* jeans?" The answers likely are, "Because everyone else is doing it, wearing it, and talking about it."

The problem is that peer-pressure decisions are based on the standards of the group. Teenagers will violate their own principles and morals to be accepted by the group. There are many more followers than leaders, and peer pressure brings out the follower in all of us.

Kids who make decisions based solely on emotion are not rare either. Emotional acts are passionate and impulsive, and it is hard to explain "why" you did something when it was an emotional act.

At one school two young women had a big term paper to write. Both were feeling overwhelmed with the project and their lack of preparation, so on the spur of the moment they emptied their bank accounts, took $400, and flew to Los Angeles. It was a simple, emotional decision.

It is a rare teenager who makes purely logical decisions, although in extreme cases students may try to do this out of overwhelming emotional hurt. To a degree this is how we want to teach our children to reach decisions, but teenagers are often not mature enough to weigh other important decision-making factors, such as ethics, morals, and the long-term consequences of their actions.

One young woman, Tammie, made the decision to commit suicide based on logical but skewed reasoning. Tammie's father was sexually abusing her, and she reasoned that if she told her mother about it, it would cause her mom grief, her parents would probably divorce, and a divorce would affect Tammie's other siblings. Moreover, Tammie's father was a successful businessman, and chances were good that the abuse would become public knowledge. Then her father's business would fail, and the rest of the family would be affected financially as well. But if Tammie killed herself instead, she reasoned, her mother would grieve but she'd eventually recover, and the rest of the family would remain intact.

There was no arguing with her logic. It was well thought out, and her conclusions were probably accurate. But Tammie did not consider the ethics of the situation. To do so was beyond her maturation level. In spite of logic, there was no way I could let her follow through with her conclusion.

By law I have to report sexual abuse to an authority. I did, Tammie's father was arrested, and I met the mother, father, and Tammie at the police station. The father was very angry and threatened everyone with libel suits. I told him that no matter whether the charges were true or false, the least he could do as a parent was to get Tammie some counseling. "If the charges are true," I said, "this child needs professional help. If they are not true and she has made all this up, she still needs professional help." Tammie got the help she needed.

You must try to understand where your kids are coming from when they make a decision. Ask what decisions your children are making, and then examine how they arrived at their choices. For example, if a student is shoplifting, the parent should try to discover what is happening in the teen's life to cause them to shoplift. Is there pressure from friends? Are they expressing an emotional hurt? Or do they need something from the store they cannot buy? When kids make bad decisions, correct them, and teach them why the decision was faulty.

Love and Respect Must be Communicated

There are innumerable ways of showing love and respect for one another. Most of them take a little extra time and thought, but they pay back hefty dividends in terms of healthier, more open relationships. Teens, tell your parents that you love and respect them. Parents, tell your kids that you love and respect them.

Communicate. "You don't understand me" is a shutdown in communication, and problems can *only* be resolved when you talk about them. If a teenager can't communicate verbally with a parent, it is the fault of the parent, simply because parents are the mature party whose responsibility it is to open communication.

When verbal communication is impossible, either the parents or the teenager should try to communicate by writing. Paul Horne had difficulty saying verbally how he felt, but he did write it down.

Here are some guidelines for parents and kids when writing letters to each other: Never attack. Begin your letter with love and respect. Explain what you are doing and why. "I have difficulty talking, so I'm writing." Use specific examples of the problems. Write concisely, logically, and lovingly. Sometimes it helps to get the anger out of your system by writing a letter that no one will ever see, destroying the first letter, and writing another that follows the above rules.

Hand the letter to the addressee when they will have a chance to read it in private and react in private. The recipient needs time to think over the contents. Build your communication through letters, and then move to verbal communication.

Express love. We all need to hear it, feel it, and say it daily. Expressed love builds self-esteem, security, and confidence. Love is healing. When trust is violated, it takes love and patience for trust to be reestablished. If everyone were to get the love and respect they need from their families, overcrowded prisons, gang violence, drug use, and teen pregnancies would be a thing of the past. Love and respect start at home.

Questions and Answers

1. Do I have to say "I love you?" That's hard for me to say.

I'll answer that with a story. An old farmer and his wife had been married 40 years. One day the wife got upset and told her husband she wanted to go to marriage counseling. When they went the wife explained to the counselor, "My husband never tells me he loves me."

The farmer replied, "Well, I told her I loved her 40 years ago. When I change my mind I'll let her know."

Of course you need to say "I love you." How else is your loved one going to know how you feel? I don't know anyone who doesn't want to be loved, and saying "I love you" reinforces positive feelings. People need to be built up emotionally, and those three little words, "I love you," are critically important emotional feeding.

Besides, the more you say it, it the easier it comes. The same is true of compliments; the more you practice, the easier they are to give and receive.

2. Shouldn't my kids know I love them because of all the things I do for them?

No, all human beings—and, yes, teens fall under that category—need to be told constantly that they're loved and lovable. They need it demonstrated. Kids need the hugs, they need the words, they need the kisses, and they need the strokes. After all, if a cook works all day in the kitchen fixing a meal, the meal is eaten, and no one tells the cook how much it was enjoyed, how can the cook know his or her efforts are appreciated? We all need positive strokes, and saying "I love you" is one of the best positive strokes we can give or get.

3. Can I love my kids too much?

You can't love kids too much, but you can be too protective. Your teenagers will let you know if you're too protective; they'll tell you, "Just let me try it myself!"

4. Respect is just a joke at our house. My kids talk back. They ignore me. I don't even know where to begin.

Call the family together and state, without yelling and screaming, that the situation has to change. From that point on, everyone in the family must be treated with respect, which means no more put-downs, name calling, and physical or verbal assaults. These rules have to be enforced from the top down. Parents have to abide by the rules so that the kids will also follow them.

Next, there have to be consequences for violating someone's "civil rights." People have the right to be at home without being called names, lambasted, beaten up, or ignored. Stick to the consequences when the rules are broken.

5. My teenagers act as if they don't even like me. How are they supposed to respect me?

Ask your kids why they don't respect you. Kids have reasons. Ask them why they act and feel the way they do, and they'll tell you. I've had teens tell me that they mistreat their parents because it is the only way they can get attention, because they don't want to be ignored, or because they're hurting and want to lash out at someone else. Ask.

6. What's the difference between respect and obedience?

Anyone can be made to obey if you apply enough force. But if people are taught respect, they'll be obedient because they respect the authority. Respect is earned through the rightful authority it represents.

I want my kids to obey me because they respect me, and I want them to respect me because they know I'm not going to ask them to do something wrong, harmful, or hurtful. I look out for their best interests and good. Then my children will be obedient, not because they're forced to be obedient, but because they love me and understand why I do what I do.

7. You want us to care about how our children think and feel, but my kids don't care how I think or feel.

You are the adult. The child is the child. The point is that it isn't what your child can do for you, it is what you can do for your child. Recently a school counselor told me that she called up a parent to tell her that her daughter was very depressed. The mother's reaction was, "Well, what does she have to be depressed about? I'm the one who's depressed!" Remember, you're the parent. It's your responsibility to take care of your child, not vice versa.

Teaching a child how to care begins with parents demonstrating that they care for the child. If your children don't care about your feelings, make them aware of what you feel and why. Teach them to consider what they say and do in light of how it affects others.

8. Why should I explain what is expected of my children? Shouldn't they know what I want?

Why should they know? That's a common mistake everyone makes: If I know, everybody knows. But it's not true. Kids are not born with instincts automatically telling them what is expected of them. They need to be taught and trained.

When I went to boot camp, I had an idea about what was expected of me, but I didn't know specifically what to do. I knew I was supposed to march, but when you throw 180 guys together and say "march," there are a lot of unanswered questions. Where are they supposed to stand? What foot do they start out with? What rhythm are they supposed to walk in? How long a step do they take?

Just because I had a general idea of what was expected didn't mean I understood the specifics. I had to be taught. Children also need to be taught the specifics.

9. If kids need boundaries, how come they're always pushing against them?

Young people push so they can find out if there are really boundaries and if they hold up under pressure. Kids push to see what will happen if they cross the line.

Kids *should* test their boundaries. We don't want to raise a bunch of sheep. Think of how much the human race has gained by pushing back our boundaries. For hundreds of years we tested the boundary of flight. Flying was "impossible" for man, but there were always people testing that premise. Finally the Wright brothers succeeded in pushing the boundary back forever at Kitty Hawk.

As children grow they become more mature and more able to handle responsibility, so we remove, or move back, some of their boundaries. There are always boundaries that should never be crossed, such as drug use. Generally, however, a boundary should be flexible so it can grow and change with the child.

10. Why do my children ignore me or do the opposite of what I tell them?

You teach children tasks, but in the heart of every child is foolishness. That's part of being a kid. You teach your children to brush their teeth, and without exception when you ask, they'll tell you they forgot. You have to keep telling them until they gain the responsibility and ability to take care of themselves.

When my daughter Heidi was 13, my son Matthew, 11, and my daughter, Hannah, eight, they each had their own ideas about taking care of themselves. Heidi was very big on hygiene. She kept her clothes clean, washed her hair, and took good care of herself. Hannah had nearly reached that stage, too.

But Matthew, who was three years older than Hannah, was a total slob. To him a pair of blue jeans, tennis shoes, and a T-shirt were high fashion. And just because he'd worn them four days in a row didn't mean he couldn't wear them four more. As long as his socks didn't crunch when he put them on in the morning, he assumed they were still clean.

I'm exaggerating, but the point is that I'd taught all my kids about personal hygiene, but until they'd matured to a point where it became important to them, I had to stay after them. For Heidi and Hannah, it came early; for Matthew it came a little later. But it did come, and it became important to him also.

Kids won't ignore you forever. Sooner or later your teaching will kick in.

Teenagers also do the opposite of what their parents say or do because they are becoming their own person. Perhaps you've taught your kids to go to church every Sunday. Undoubtedly, at some time during their high school or college years, they will rebel against going to church. That is because they want to make up their own minds about what they do or do not believe. If your values are being challenged, don't give up. It may be comforting to know that eventually your children will come back to the values and morals they were taught as kids.

11.   I don't believe I should teach my kids about morality. I believe that we each need to find our own morals.

It seems to me that this is saying you aren't going to give your children any boundaries, you're just going to let them run wild. Would you do that when they want to drive a car? Would you give them the keys and let them learn how to drive on their own with no regard for the rules of the road?

Morality is society's boundaries, its rules of the road, and morals must be taught just as driving is taught. Society sets moral boundaries so people cannot rape, rob, or murder without the consequence of punishment. Without these boundaries there would not be society, there would be chaos. If you don't give your children moral boundaries, you are asking them to deal with chaos.

9

Balance and Self-Esteem

"I really get depressed at times.
I don't believe in God, not anymore anyway."
— from "Who Am I?" essay by Paul Horne

Teens Need Balance in Life

All human beings have four basic areas of need. Every thing we desire and require falls into one of four categories: physical, mental, emotional, and spiritual. For good health you must fulfill all these needs and keep them in balance, just as your diet must be kept in balance. Everyone knows that you can't eat only protein. Your body needs vegetables, fruit, grains and other carbohydrates, and dairy products as well. Similarly, man can't live solely on mental, physical, emotional, or spiritual stimulation. When he tries, the other areas of need go unfulfilled, and major problems occur.

First are the physical needs. These include shelter, food, water, and clothing. In most parts of the world a person who is missing any one of these essentials will soon die.

Second are mental needs. We need mental stimulation. A young mother who is home all day with toddlers is a good example of this. She gears herself to the mentality of her little children. She talks baby talk, reads Dr. Seuss, and watches "Sesame Street." After a few hours of this, she can't wait until an adult comes over so she can think and speak like an adult.

Third, are emotional needs. We need to love and be loved, to respect and be respected. If we are not loved or respected at home, we start looking elsewhere for something to fill that need. Too many people are unhappy because they have not found love or respect in their lives.

Fourth are spiritual needs. Many people benefit from having a relationship with God or — as Alcoholics Anonymous terms it — some form of Higher Power. Many people don't want to recognize this as a need, but when they are put into a time of crisis — no matter who they are and no matter what they believe — most will call out for spiritual comfort.

All four of these areas are crucial to our existence, and that is why it is important to maintain them in balance in our lives. Balancing the mental, physical, emotional, and spiritual is not easy. In this society we put strong emphasis on two areas of need and let the other two areas go by the wayside. Emphasis is placed primarily on physical and mental needs, and much less on emotional and spiritual needs. Any time something gets out of balance it doesn't run well — including human beings. In the long run a lack of balance drags a person down, and depression is a likely result. Let's look at each area to see how it is emphasized or neglected.

Physical Needs

In this country we stress physical abilities. We spend tons of money to watch professional athletes whose bodies are in tip-top condition. A hot college athlete can practically write his own multimillion-dollar contract into the pros. Betting on sports

— from football to horse racing — is a national hobby. The Olympics keep millions of people glued to their television sets. We revel in all levels of sport from Little League to the Super Bowl.

Tons more money is spent by everyday participants. Sports and exercise are big business. There are special equipment, clothes, and shoes to buy. On top of that we spend billions of dollars a year going on diets and joining health clubs, to try to become or stay physically fit. As a nation our physical ideal is to be young, healthy, and athletic.

The reason it is important to maintain our physical being is evident when people don't take care of themselves. They get out of shape and are more susceptible to illness. Obesity has been linked to an increased risk of certain kinds of cancer, high blood pressure, and heart disease. Two-thirds of all deaths in the United States are due to heart attacks, stroke, or cancer, all of which preventable to some degree by watching our diets and exercising regularly.

Heart attacks kill more than half a million people in the United States each year. Another one million will live through their heart attacks. More than 50 percent of the country's population is at risk for stroke or coronary disease, and one in four will die of cancer. Increasingly researchers are finding that diet and exercise can prevent many of these diseases. The side effects of lack of exercise and poor eating habits are expensive and lethal.

Lately there has also been a focus on cigarette smoking. Everyone has heard for years that smoking is bad for you. It is not just unhealthy, it is deadly. Surgeon General C. Everett Koop released a report in 1988 stating that more than 300,000 people a year die from the side effects of smoking, some of whom die from breathing other people's cigarette fumes!

I want to emphasize that we should stay healthy and keep our bodies in the best possible condition. We should be concerned about diet and exercise. Yet this physical focus, sometimes bordering on obsession, is evidence that our society is wrapped up in the physical aspects of life.

Mental Needs

We also emphasize mental abilities. We send our kids to schools where they are pressured to excel. In today's school system students are expected to learn more, and more quickly, than did their parents. When I was in kindergarten the time was spent mainly in coloring, playing with blocks, and eating graham-cracker snacks. My daughter began to learn how to read when she was in kindergarten. I had to know my multiplication tables by fifth grade. My son had to know his multiplication tables by third grade.

When I was in high school an electric typewriter was available only at the richest corporations. Now our five- and six-year-olds play with computers in the classroom. Whiz kids who break into the computer industry with a new product earlier than anyone else suddenly become fantastically rich. They are on the cutting edge of technology and knowledge. Parents want that for their kids too! Parents feel the anxiety of being behind accelerating technology, and they pressure their kids to stay ahead.

Next, we emphasize the "right" schools and entrance exams for college. Every year the newspapers report how each state compares with the others on exam scores. We tell our kids that where they go to school can make a difference in their future. If you want to "become," you must get a certain score on your test so you can go to a certain university, get your degree with a grade-point average high enough to get into the right graduate school, and finish early so you'll be offered The Job. We haven't become as obsessed as some countries, where toddlers practice so they can score well on the test to get into an elite preschool, which will get them into an elite kindergarten, which will get them into an elite elementary school, which will . . . , but American kids are being forced to think about their "future" at younger and younger ages.

There is a strong emphasis placed on mental ability, and students are pressured from kindergarten through graduate school, because we admire mental strength.

Emotional Needs

The emotional aspect of life is often terribly lacking. If the physical and mental are overemphasized, the emotional and the spiritual undoubtedly suffer. It takes strong emotional character for kids to be able to cope with the pressure of physical and mental demands. And if young people enter adolescence unbalanced — tipped too much toward athletics or academics — the pressure and stress of being a teen weigh even more heavily on them. This pressure can cause teenagers to turn to drugs and alcohol. This lack of emotional maturity also leads to pregnancy and other "teen problems," because kids try to cope from an unbalanced position.

There are several reasons today's kids struggle emotionally more than their parents did. The stress of being a teenager is phenomenal. A lot of parents think that when they were in school things were tough. They also tend to believe that today's schools are similar to the ones they went to 20 or 30 years ago. But the situations kids face in public school today are different from those of their parents.

For teenagers in the '50s, life wasn't perfect, but a naivete surround this peaceful decade. Just watch a "Leave It to Beaver" episode if you don't think this is true. In the '60s teens matured with the political unrest of the Vietnam War and the hippie movement of drug use and free love. But kids in the '60s were more tolerant than modern teens. After all, the counterculture said everyone had the right to do his or her own thing.

The '70s were a period of disillusionment. Virtually everyone recognized that the Vietnam War was a terrible waste of youthful lives. The idea that drugs "expanded" the mind gave way to tragic stories of overdoses and ruined lives. And "free" love turned out to cost a lot when babies were added to the picture. It was during the '70s that the teen suicide rate began to increase rapidly.

Today far fewer kids are accepted by their peers than during the '50s, '60s, and even '70s, especially at school. There is a clear distinction between cliques — stoners, eggheads, jocks, preppies. Whatever the label, more kids are *not* being accepted than are being accepted. To be accepted by one group is to be rejected by the others, so no matter what teens do, they set themselves up for rejection, and rejection takes a lot of courage to overcome. We seem to have become a more critical society, and this takes a big emotional toll.

Next on the list of pressures facing today's teens is home life. Very few adults grew up in single-parent homes. Divorce carried such a social stigma that unhappy couples just gritted their teeth and somehow lived through bad situations.

Today, a couple that makes it through 15 years of marriage is a statistical anomaly. Divorce is so socially acceptable that it is sometimes used as an easy way out rather than as a last resort. This means that kids often don't have the stable environment they need to grow up emotionally strong in this shaky world. It is not that single parents and divorced families can't make young people feel emotionally secure, but that they don't have someone with whom to share the responsibility.

Kids always need to know that their lives are safe and secure. This goes beyond having two parents in the same house. Kids like to have the security of their own room and bed, their place at the table, and their limits. They need to know that the bills are paid, that there will continue to be a roof over their heads, and that one of their parents will be there to take care of them. These things give them a firm emotional foundation.

In addition, young people want to know that they are loved,

and they must know what is expected of them. Some parents think that giving kids freedom to do whatever they want is an expression of love. I disagree. If you let teens do anything they want, any time they want, you aren't showing them they are loved, you are showing them that you don't care. In my experience, parents who care set boundaries. That too provides emotional security, because kids then know where and how they fit into their family and society.

Emotional security is also difficult to maintain because families are much more mobile these days. Every time kids change schools, they have to start developing friendships all over. If your family moves, you have to work harder to make your children feel secure in the one environment that remains constant — their family. This is important, because only when a young person has a strong base of emotional support at home are they comfortable enough to be themselves, rather than being what someone else wants them to be.

Emotional support provided at home gives kids the strength to resist peer pressure. I was taught by my parents not to be bigoted. And I felt secure enough saying "no" when bigotry was expressed by my friends, because I knew my beliefs were backed up at home. That gave me the emotional support to speak out against something I knew was wrong.

One difference I see between leaders and followers is that leaders have enough confidence in their emotional support that they dare to stand up and voice an opinion. Not everyone can be a leader; certainly there are born leaders. Yet even teens who are not born leaders can be led only as far as their concepts of what is right and wrong, *if* they have a strong emotional base. When parents provide kids with a solid emotional foundation, youths are confident enough to be themselves.

It is true that the emotional aspects of our lives are usually undernurtured. Parents can prevent their children's emotional starvation by providing support and stability, keeping boundaries strong and consistent, and loving their children endlessly and unconditionally.

Spiritual Needs

Spiritual development is equally as important but as neglected as emotional development. I feel that people need to
know God. I believe we are created by God and that all of us
want to have a personal relationship with Him.

It is obvious to me that humans need to have a spiritual
relationship, because everywhere I look I see people fascinated
with the spiritual. Religion is in the news every day. Millions
have traveled thousands of miles, suffered incredible hard-
ships, and even died for their beliefs. Although there may be
only a handful of "major" religions, there are dozens of religious denominations branching off from each of these, and it
often seems that everyone has his or her individual beliefs
about God.

Teenagers get confused about issues of religion, church, and
spirituality. Paul Horne is an example of a teen who had a
somewhat dfferent view of God as shown in his essay "Who
Am I?" at the end of this book.

I believe that although Paul was not developing spiritually,
there was a part of him that longed to be. Many kids have little
or no spiritual upbringing, but like Paul, they desire to know
spiritual things. I'm not going to tell people what to believe,
and there are many ways to teach spirituality outside an organ-
ized church. But I do believe that the message of God is vital in
the lives of adolescents — and all others, for that matter.

When a person has made an ethical or moral mistake of such
magnitude that his or her life can only go forward with a totally
fresh start, a belief in God can be invaluable. Earlier I talked
about Michelle, a young woman who went to a party and lost
her virginity and reputation because of the mistakes she made.
When I talked to Michelle, she was very depressed, and the
only thing I could say that mattered to her was that God would

forgive her. This forgiveness was what Michelle needed. She could start over, and because she had forgiveness, she was able to hold her head up and reestablish the reputation she wanted. Michelle was able to put the incident behind her.

Spirituality is vitally important to all of us. But because we don't die if we forget about it for a few weeks or years, it is often ignored or pushed back to worry about "later." Yet an underemphasis of the spiritual is making youth more vulnerable to all the worldly problems. Humans have to believe in something. Spirituality gives their lives an underpinning, a support, that is impossible to find anywhere else. Start listening to those who are successful, be they athletes or actors, politicians or physicians. You'll hear people saying in many ways that they owe it all to God and this truth can be helpful to teenagers along with the emotional, physical, and mental lessons.

The Consequences of Imbalance

Many teenagers don't have much of a spiritual or emotional base to work from; therefore, they make decisions from an unbalanced state that can be dangerous. Seventeen-year-old Tammie, whom we met in Chapter 8, had decided to commit suicide because she was being sexually abused. She reviewed the facts, considered the consequences, and made the decision from a purely logical, mental perspective. Did her careful logic make it the right decision? Absolutely not. She arrived at the wrong decision because she was unbalanced. Just like many other people in this society, Tammie was more mentally and physically oriented than spiritually and emotionally oriented.

She did not take into consideration the spiritual issue of right and wrong. Her abuser was wrong, but Tammie wasn't wrong. Making a decision from a purely mental approach left out the moral part of the equation. It was morally wrong for Tammie to kill herself, but she didn't consider that — again, because she had little spiritual background.

Emotionally, Tammie didn't take into account that she mattered, that she was important, and that she should love herself. When she only thought her problem through mentally, she drew the wrong conclusions.

There are other typical ways that kids get in trouble when they make decisions from only one perspective. If on a warm spring day two teenagers, newly in love, find themselves parked in a secluded spot, it is easy to make a decision to have sex, because physically it seems like the only decision to make. But if these kids decide to have sex based on their physical needs alone, they chance becoming more emotionally involved than they may have planned, and they risk an unplanned pregnancy. Quite often unbalanced decisions end up costing a lot.

It is also not unheard of to make decisions based solely on spiritual beliefs. That's what produces religious zealots. Consider terrorists, who view the world only from their religious perspective, and all the lives that have been lost fighting over religious territory. Mentally these "warriors" can justify their actions: It's a ugly world anyway; what's one more bomb, or one more life? Terrorists apparently don't look at the destruction they cause emotionally, and they obviously don't worry about the pain and grief of the victims and their families, because spiritually they believe they are assuring their place with their God. This is an extreme example of a decision skewed toward one aspect, but it costs thousands of lives yearly, all in the name of religion.

Faulty decisions are made from an overemphasis on one area or from a lack of development or maturity in others, usually emotional or spiritual. Over and over, teenagers, usually girls, tell me they are sexually active because they're afraid that if they refuse sex to their partners, their partners will leave them. These teens are lacking emotionally and are using sex to fill the gap.

My friend Dennis hurt because he didn't have emotional support from his parents. Instead of reaching out to someone else for the support he needed, he reached out to narcotics. Drugs masked his pain.

I see this again and again. If teenagers have problems and they don't have emotional or spiritual strength to draw on, they go on tilt like a pinball machine. They look for a way out, and that way is readily available through narcotics. Kids often turn to drugs because it is easier to get stoned than to deal with the issues. They can pretend they don't care.

Paul Horne lacked emotionally, too. In his essay he wrote, "All the years that I've been in school, I've never had a girl-friend who has really liked me. I always wonder what I'm doing wrong. I'm a nice, understanding person. I don't know why they won't give me a chance. I've always wanted to meet a special person who would care about me and love me and I could love and care about her." He had an emotional need that wasn't being met, and it contributed to his depression.

Whenever a decision is made solely from an overwhelming physical urge, a mental belief, a religious conviction, or an emotional impulse, or because of a need in one of these areas, that decision is made from an unbalanced position. The decision won't work. The only way to reach the right solution to a problem is to draw from a balanced position.

Learning Balance

Young people should be cared for and taught to care for all aspects of their being. When they are small they have to be cared for physically — taken to the doctor for vaccinations, fed healthy food, and encouraged to exercise — so they stay healthy and grow. As they get older we teach them to do these things for themselves. Then we send them to school to gain mental strength and stimulation. But that isn't all that kids need. Young people also need to be loved and nurtured so they can grow emotionally and they need a spiritual understanding. That is what I mean by balance.

The problems I see among kids occur when they don't have that balance and respond accordingly. Young adults who operate within a framework of physical, mental, emotional, and spiritual balance make it through their teenage years more happily and successfully.

Self-Esteem

Self-esteem or self-worth is the way we see and value ourselves. Young people develop self-esteem based on what their parents, grandparents, role models, and friends value. For example, if you compliment your children on good grades or even-temperedness, or if their peers think they are good in athletics or poised in speaking, they will highly value those traits and accomplishments because their family or peers value them.

For this reason, self-esteem can be easily misdirected, especially when one is young and immature. Teenagers look at themselves through other people's eyes. Thus they forget or were never taught to like themselves because they are good, worthy people, and to value their unique traits because *they* like them. Similar to being thrown out of balance by paying too much attention to one aspect of life or neglecting another, self-esteem placed with the wrong emphasis can result in self-doubts, self-hatred, and a negative self-image.

It's no wonder that esteem based on one's academic records, personal appearance, charm, or athletic ability causes problems. People who base their self-worth on these transitory things will find that the time comes when they aren't successful at what other people want them to be. Everyone fails. One sign of depression is a constant feeling of worthlessness or self-hatred. It's a signal that an individual's self-esteem is slipping. That's when the "I hate" attitude begins. Let's look at some examples of poor and misplaced self-esteem and how they affect an individual.

Low Self-Esteem

Low self-esteem seems to be epidemic. Adolescents with low self-esteem put themselves down, they put others down, they say "I hate" a lot, and they express dissatisfaction with virtually everything — their looks, their school performance, their family, their friends, and their life. The problem is that poor self-esteem feeds on itself. Once you start talking about how bad things are, they stay bad or even get worse. This is positive affirmation in reverse. If you say bad things about yourself over and over, the statements become self-fulfilling.

When teens' self-worth is low they get depressed, and depressed kids do desperate things. As a result, often they find themselves in situations that seem hopeless. They get hooked on drugs or alcohol, they get pregnant, they contract venereal diseases, and they continue to be very unhappy. The more depressed kids get, the more endless the problems seem. It is hard to like yourself when everything you touch seems to be rotten.

Bad things also happen to good kids because they don't have the self-esteem to resist peer pressure. Girls and boys give themselves sexually and use drugs because they don't believe in themselves enough to say, "No thanks, I don't need that."

If teens learned to value themselves as good people in their own right, it wouldn't matter whether or not everyone else was "doing it" or "using it." If they didn't want to "do it," they wouldn't. Kids with healthy self-esteem can do, say, and be just who they are. Healthy self-esteem lets the *individual* make the choices — not their friends, not anyone else.

Put-downs and insults are another symptom of self-hatred and low self-esteem. Kids put other kids down to try to elevate their own worth or to be funny. If they tell someone, "You're ugly," what they are saying is, "I'm better looking than you." "You're stupid" means "I'm smarter than you." Put-downs are also accepted because they often get a laugh. For example, on the television show "Cheers," most of the jokes are at the expense of someone else. And we all chuckle! If young people hear put-downs on television and then hear their parents insult others, they will learn to imitate them. How many children are told by their folks that they are ugly or dumb? The next thing those kids do is turn around and say the same thing to their little brothers or sisters. Insulting another person is a learned skill.

Self-worth built at the expense of someone else is based on a false notion. There will always be someone bigger, brighter, smarter, and badder. Insults do not elevate anyone; they hurt everyone.

Low self-esteem is a personal crisis. It is not liking yourself enough to stand up for what you know to be right and wrong. It is putting yourself or others down. Low self-esteem leads to depression, and if you already dislike yourself, it makes it much harder to recover from depression.

Misplaced Self-Esteem

Misplaced self-esteem, or investing worth in the wrong things, also causes major problems. It isn't wrong to be proud of your children's special skills. If your child is a great artist, a terrific writer, fashion model material, a fast runner, or a wonderful musician, enjoy and encourage those talents. The harm comes when pride in one aspect of a person's life becomes their focus.

Self-esteem can be improperly based on fleeting things. When parents place emphasis on the physical exterior, they overbalance children toward an aspect of themselves over which they have no control. A friend of mine who is very attractive had parents who loved dressing her up and talking about her physical beauty. Soon her entire self-worth was centered around her appearance. She grew up thinking she wasn't smart or talented, because all her self-worth was based on how she looked.

By the teen years, this focus on appearances accelerates. All the guys are interested in an attractive female — not because of her personality, intelligence, goals, hopes, or desires, but because of how a pretty she looks. This affirms the belief that outward appearance contains everything of value. The exterior becomes highly polished and the rest is left to go.

The same thing happens to males. A good-looking guy may find it's hard to remember that he has to be a good person too. Friends come around without any effort, and it is easy to discard them since there always seems to be a ready supply. Handsome young men often take advantage of girls because it is so easy to do. These teens' self-worth is wrapped up in how they look and how pretty or popular their girlfriends are, rather than in building good, lasting friendships, or being a kind and decent person. Predictably, the inner person suffers.

Teenagers and parents have to remember that there is a limit to self-worth based on a pretty or handsome face or a great body. Hollywood typifies this attitude — you are valuable when you're gorgeous and on top; get lost if you've lost your "face value." As a people gets older, they realize physical beauty will not last. Physical appearance is a terribly shaky foundation on which to build self-esteem. Those who have done so have to "re-find" themselves when their beauty fades.

Self-esteem based on physical gifts includes special athletic ability. Expectations in athletics run high, and students are quickly pushed into considering themselves "elite" or special because of physical gifts. In reality very few people make the top grade in athletics. The fall will come sooner or later.

A few years ago a young woman who was a nationally rated track athlete competed in a race. This athlete's successes were coming harder and harder as younger runners challenged her position, and she quickly fell behind in the race. Apparently distraught over her inability to win, she left the event, ran down a street, and jumped off a bridge. Her self-esteem was tied to her athletic talent. She could no longer meet her own expectations, which were tied to her ability to win races, and she was desperate enough about her "failure" to attempt suicide.

Former pro basketball player Pete Maravich once estimated that one in 12,000 basketball players makes it to the NBA. It is rare enough to be an exceptional athlete, but rarer still to find one who has moved away from the sports arena and found success in another field. Those who have possess self-worth beyond their strong physique.

Even for those who defy all odds and become "superstars," the status lasts only for a limited time. When the Boston Celtics went into the 1988 NBA Final Playoffs, a big issue was whether or not their starting five players would be able to handle the stress of the series because they were getting old. Their average age was 31.

What happens when you are a star athlete and you're suddenly dumped out into life at 32 years of age? Or when you are a star high school athlete who gets dumped at 18 and a half because in the excitement of playing sports you forgot to study? Few colleges want to recruit athletes who didn't bother to study in high school. Few businesses pay big bucks to retired athletes to wear their tennis shoes.

Over-the-hill sports figures try to regain lost self-worth by reliving their glory days. Boxers go back into the ring for one last round. Football players come out of retirement to try and make one more season. Over-the-hill high school players still hang around school one, two, or five years after their graduation. They are trying to recapture the self-worth they had for a few years on the football field, volleyball court, or baseball diamond. When self-worth is focused solely on something as temporary as physical appearance or athletic ability, people go through a major crisis as their physical gifts age.

Self-worth can be based on other things besides athletics, but any time self-worth is misguided, people set themselves up for defeat. Smart alecks may get laughs and attention in class, but no one wants to hire them once they finish school. If self-worth is based on impressing everyone that you're rough and tough, the fighter will lose over the long run, and more than just a few brawls. If you're better looking than everybody else, when the beauty fades, self-worth also fades. If self-worth is based on being the smartest person in the company, when other people start coming out of college with brighter and newer ideas, self-worth is lost.

Any time self-worth is based on things that can change, there will be an awful crash at the end. Self-worth should always be based on personal aspects that last a lifetime: honesty, trustworthiness, reliability, sincerity, friendliness, kindness, persistence, generosity, thoughtfulness, and cheerfulness. Praise your children for these accomplishments, and their self-esteem will be strong and stay strong even when everything else around them changes. Some ways to keep your children's self-image strong follow.

Building Self-Esteem

1. Treat your children as you want to be treated.
2. Find at least one positive thing to say to your children each day.
3. Offer your kids a chance to succeed by having many different kinds of activities for them to try.
4. Recognize effort made, not just perfect results.
5. Listen to your kids, answer their questions openly and honestly, and encourage them to be proud of themselves, their ideas, and their work.
6. Emphasize what your kids do right, instead of what they do wrong.
7. Keep goals for kids within their reach.
8. Pass out compliments for creativity — for coming up with new ideas, trying something different, or improving on everyday tasks.
9. Make your children feel that they belong, and never embarrass them, especially in front of others.

It's easy for me to tell you how to build your child's self-esteem in the right way, but it's also easy for parents to put too much emphasis on the wrong things. To avoid misguiding your children's self-esteem, examine your motives. Why do you want your kids to succeed? Because you will have bragging rights, or because you want them to do and be the best they can? Expectations of success should be our children's, not ours.

I do expect my children to work as hard as they can at whatever they undertake. But if they work hard and the results are that they aren't the top of the class, the best ballet dancer, or the star soccer player, that's all right with them and with me.

Although it is natural for parents to want their kids to do and be the best — it makes you look good, too — you have to be careful. I'd like all my kids to have 4.0 grade-point averages in school. It'd sure make me feel smart! But I'm a realist and I know that a 4.0 GPA is the exception, not the rule. To expect my kids to get "A's" in every subject is not realistic.

Instead, we should teach our kids to do the very best they can. If the best they can do in gym class is a "C," they shouldn't be pressured to get an "A" just because we think there is no value in a lesser grade. But if they can get an "A" in math, then they should be expected to get an "A." Parents have to be aware of their child's individual abilities. Then they will know when to praise a "C" grade, and when to say that a "B" is not up to par.

Parents with unrealistic expectations and values can do harm to their children. We lived near a family that had two children — a son and a daughter — and this family had the most misguided expectations and motives I have ever seen. They looked good enough. These kids wore the best clothes, their yard was always carefully manicured, and the cars were nearly spotless. Everything was always totally perfect. But this was so because to this family, appearances were all-important. Their self-worth as a family was dependent on the appearance of their home, possessions, and children.

Their son and daughter were taught that self-worth revolved around the clothes they wore, the bikes they rode, and the tennis shoes they owned, not in how they acted. The parents so emphasized the way things looked that they completely neglected their children's character. The kids came over to my house so they could act like children. They came over to get dirty and make a mess.

Think about how those kids felt. They could never do things right. It was impossible for them to be perfect — there is always one hair, one eyelash, or one piece of dust in the wrong place. They could never do things wrong. They couldn't act like real kids, because that would make them dirty and take away from their "perfection." Their parents' love and value of them was based on how they looked, not on what kind of people they were. These children may have looked perfect, but they were miserable. Self-esteem in this family was completely misplaced.

Encourage artistic talent, physical ability, and mental strength in your kids, but place the most value on characteristics that show "being": being loving, kind, generous, sensitive to others, honest, thoughtful, and moral. These traits are lasting.

The only realistic thing any of us can base self-worth on is the inner self, the one personal aspect worth valuing. The inner self is present when you're a child, it is present when you're middle-aged, and it is present when you're old. Self-esteem shouldn't be built on temporary qualities that lose their importance and disappear in time.

If you value people for their inner abilities, they will develop a sense of worth that becomes part of them. In all young people you can find at least one thing worth praising. They will become proud of that aspect of their personality, and it will develop and mature. Parents have to zero in on the person inside, looking beyond accomplishments and defeats.

Value and Character

I believe that one of the reasons self-esteem is low in so many people is that values have changed. In this country, honesty is no longer considered admirable. Even our role models aren't honest. Politicians are often less than truthful; it seems as if the best liars gets elected. Lawyers have a general reputation of being out to get whatever they can for themselves and their clients, with facts being secondary to the bottom line.

While honesty is not valued, cheating and lying have become acceptable traits, because the people doing them are making big bucks, and big bucks are one thing this society *does* value. Periodically the stock market reels with convictions for insider trading, and drug dealers are among the country's richest citizens. Even at home, people cheat on their income tax.

We have lost old-fashioned values. The emphasis has switched from honesty and integrity to making money, no matter what the moral price. When kids look to their parents and see that self-worth depends on the size of a house or the make of a car rather than on moral principles and character, they too develop their self-worth in those directions.

Our society also equates fame with value. We lift mere mortals to great heights because they are entertainers. John Belushi was a famous comedian, but fame didn't get him too far. He died of a drug overdose. Elvis Presley, Janis Joplin, Jimi Hendrix, and dozens of others were admired by millions, but all overdosed on drugs and died. Yet we still exalt these people. Our young adults have to be taught to evaluate people for their character. They must learn that what makes a person good or valuable to society is not money, looks, or talent.

Teenagers' self-worth and esteem are based on societal standards and their parent's self-worth and values. The danger today is that strength of character has lost value with nearly everyone. Character is important because in a time of crisis, the only tangible evidence of self-worth is character. I would choose character over popularity any day, because character stands against popular opinion. Today most people in Germany are ashamed of the history of their actions during World War II. Even those who didn't participate in the death camps turned their backs on what was happening. It was popular to persecute the Jews, and it was not popular to speak out. Few Germans stood up to Hitler, because he was popular. They chose popularity over character.

I sometimes wonder if the United States has any more character than did Nazi Germany. Is there character to a society in which presidential candidate Jesse Jackson has his life threatened because he's black? To many people Jackson doesn't have a viable opinion or even a right to live, simply because of his skin color! Do we have character in a country where the importance of the dollar is almighty? Kids turn to selling drugs, even though they cause misery, pain, and death, because it is profitable. Companies sell defective products and shamelessly pollute the environment, because they make more money than if they made the products right and cleaned up after themselves.

Emphasis must return to character. Honesty is more important than profit. Kindness is more important than popularity. As parents and teachers, we must shift the emphasis back to behavior instead of material accomplishments. A person's character, honesty, self-control, and kindness must be given more value. The only way to redevelop character in our country is through transmission from parent to child. Kids need to be taught that other people have feelings, other people have rights, and that considering others' feelings and rights will reap rewards much more valuable than any amount of money.

Young people also need to be taught about what they have to be grateful for. During adolescence, a naturally self-absorbed time, kids need to look beyond their own concerns. Have your teenagers volunteer at a hospital, rest home, or community center, or work with disadvantaged kids. One of the best ways for any of us to learn appreciation for what we have is to help someone else.

Helping others also helps us build character. Character is tangible evidence that we are good, strong people who will choose right over wrong even in the most trying times. Character supports strong self-esteem, and good self-esteem is what kids need to get them through their tough adolescent years. There's a famous quotation about character: "Character is what you do when no one else is around."

Being a good person is more valuable than owning wealth. Being a good person is more valuable than being good-looking or having athletic ability. Being a good person, having character, and having healthy self-esteem are the most valuable qualities you can have and are the most important gifts parents can give to their children.

Questions and Answers

1. If a child has genuine talent in one area, how can we give that its due and still raise a balanced child?

My daughter Hannah has a real talent for gymnastics. She gets to go to special classes, she has special equipment, and she gets to do things that the other kids don't because they don't have the same talent. But that doesn't make her so special that she isn't part of the family. Her clothes still have to be hung up, and she still has to treat everyone in the family with love and respect. Talents can be encouraged, but they shouldn't exclude kids from their family responsibilities.

Also be sure to praise your children for personal accomplishments outside their special talent. Emphasize their worth as a good and caring person, not just as a great athlete or excellent student.

2. I'm a single parent. How can I give my kids balance when our family isn't balanced?

That's a tough question. My heart goes out to single parents who are trying to be both mother and father. Even though you don't have the balance of a spouse, that doesn't mean you can't give your children balance. If I were a single mother, I would love my kids and be their authority figure, but I'd also try to find a positive male influence — a grandfather, uncle, or good friend — to give them added perspective. Likewise, single fathers should try to find a positive female influence for their children.

You have to be very careful about whom you trust your kids to, but there is a need in your children's lives for influence from both sexes.

3. How can I teach balance when I'm not in balance myself?

You *can't* do it until you are in balance yourself. If you don't have your life together, how can you tell others how to get their lives together?

If I told you I'd never been married, I didn't have any kids, and I'd never been around teenagers, but I thought these ideas I'm writing about would work, you'd throw away my book about raising kids. I know that what I'm telling you works because I'm raising kids myself and working with teenagers every day. The first thing you have to do to teach balance is to learn to be in balance yourself, so you can give your children what they need.

4. It sounds so simple. Balance must be harder than that.

Balance is not simple. Balance calls to mind the guy I saw on the "Ed Sullivan Show" when I was a kid. He had an act in which he kept plates spinning on the end of long poles. When one plate started slowing down, he'd run over and get it going. Then another plate would start to wobble. He'd run back and forth to keep all the plates going. After I saw the show I got my mom's broom and a plate and tried to make my plate spin on the end of the broom. It was a lot harder than it looked.

Maintaining personal balance is just like spinning the plates. It is not something that just happens. It is practiced and sought after every day. Being in balance is something you strive for constantly. You never get it and then say, "I've done it," because as soon as you stop, one of the plates falls.

5. How can I tell if my children are out of balance?

The same way you'd tell if you were out of balance. If you're out of balance physically, your body will let you know. If you're out of balance emotionally or spiritually, the plates start slowing down. As they start teetering, you feel bad, unhappy, or depressed, and you know that you're out of balance.

Matthew, my son, was out of balance when he told me that he thought he was stupid. Who got him out of balance? I did. How did I know he was out of balance? Because he apologized for being stupid, which meant he thought negatively of himself and had a poor self-image. These were signs that things were not right.

6. I don't have any particular religious beliefs. How do I teach spiritual values?

I know very few people who do not have any spiritual values at all. I've known people who *say* they do not have spiritual values, but as soon as a tragedy strikes they ask me to pray for them.

I have a very strong Christian belief system, and I've learned to look inside myself for these beliefs. If you question whether or not you have spiritual values, I think you first need to find out what you believe. You need to search for values internally before you can pass them on to your children.

7. Aren't schools responsible for teaching this balance and self-esteem stuff?

No. The schools' purpose is to educate, as in reading, writing, and arithmetic. They are there to teach our children in the intellectual and mental areas. Schools are not surrogate parents.

The areas of the emotion, the spirit, and the heart have to be taught at home. That's the responsibility of parents, religious institutions, and the community — not the schools. Your children take classes in math, science, English, and social studies. They do not take classes in morals, integrity, honesty, and respect. These are intangibles that must be taught outside of school.

8. I don't like myself. I have poor self-esteem. How do I teach my kids to have good self-esteem?

As I've said, you have to take care of yourself first, so you can pass those lessons on to your children. If you already have children, it's a tricky thing. You have to give your children what they need while you are getting it for yourself.

If you have poor self-esteem, think about why this may be so. Were your parents overly critical? Are you harder on yourself than you need to be? Did something happen in your life that makes it hard to like the person you are?

Deal with the old or new issues that are creating imbalance in your life. Often adults who have been sexually or physically abused as children have problems relating to their families. You have to take care first of any unresolved issues you are still carrying around. Then when you start liking yourself, you will find ways to help your children like themselves also.

9. What are some other ways to build self-esteem in my children?

The most productive way is to speak positively to them. Give them compliments and recognize their talents and accomplishments. When you speak positively to them — they are good; they are important; they are loved; they can do, be, and accomplish — they'll believe you because kids believe what they are told. If you tell your child that he's pathetic, no good, and a burden, he's going to believe that.

Recognize the things your children do that are worth praising and make sure you tell them what you saw. Give them tangibles that let them know they have the capability to be honest, hardworking, and persistent:

"You told the truth even when it was hard to do."

"You finished weeding the garden even when you really wanted to be riding your bicycle."

"You tried really hard today when you were stuck on that math problem."

Self-esteem can be built. Put good in, get good out. We bake a cake with flour, butter, eggs, and sugar, and we get a cake. But if we try to bake a cake with dirt, mud, and rocks, we get a mud pie.

Remember, it is not just the ingredients that are important; the temperature is also crucial. You can't put in all the right ingredients and then turn the oven up to broil to get the cake done faster. I was turning the oven up on my son Matthew with the tone of voice I used when I reprimanded him for not taking care of himself. It destroyed his self-esteem. Just as with a cake, everything you say to your children has to work together to get the right results.

10. My child has been sexually abused, and we're dealing with that. How do I build her self-esteem?

Use the same method I described above. Use lots of positive, reinforcing statements that tell her you love her. Let her know that although something bad happened, she is lovable and you still care for her. Make sure that she recognizes that you do not blame her for the abuse.

Gresham Union High School

Let me say something. In the last hour and a half we've said a lot of things, told a lot of stories, and given some information, and if you've missed everything I've said up to this time, that's all right.

But if you miss what I'm going to say in the next five minutes, you're going to miss the entire reason I came to your school. You're going to miss one of the most valuable lessons you'll learn in your entire life, and you're going to miss the one thing you can do most of all to prevent teen suicide and, for that matter, hurts in general. So I want everyone to focus on what I have to say.

I have four children, like I said earlier, and my oldest daughter is named Heidi. Heidi is one of those kids who has always loved school. She gets good grades, she's in track, she works in the student store, she was on the Safety Patrol, she's in school choir, she's in the plays, she does everything. She is very social, and she just loves school. When she's sick we have to make her stay home.

In third grade Heidi came home from school one day and said, "Daddy, I need to talk to you." She looked really sad.

"O.K.," I said, "do you want to talk now?"

"No," said Heidi, "I want to talk to you alone."

So after dinner we went in her bedroom. I sat her down and asked, "What's wrong, honey?"

She started crying and said, "Daddy, I don't want to go to school anymore."

"What's wrong, Heidi? You like school. You've always loved it. What's wrong? Is someone being mean to you?"

"No, Daddy," she said, "nobody's being mean to me. But everybody is being mean to Gary."

Gary was a little boy in her classroom whose family didn't take very good care of him. He wore dirty clothes to school, and he wore the same clothes two, three, four days in a row. I remember one time I saw him and you could see where he had tried to comb his hair in the front, but the back was matted where he'd slept on it. Whoever his parents were, they weren't taking care of him.

I asked, "What do you mean, everybody picks on Gary?"

"Dad, everybody tells him he's dirty and he stinks. No one will sit by him at lunch and no one wants to play with him at recess. And today, Dad, everybody picked on him so much he started to cry."

It made me mad. I said, "Did they leave him alone then?"

"No, Dad. Then they all started laughing at him and calling him a crybaby."

"Do you want me to go down there and talk to those kids?" I asked.

Heidi panicked. "No Dad! Please don't, Dad, because if you do they'll start picking on me! Please don't!"

I said, "O. K., Heidi, settle down. All right, let me just pray with you about it," and I prayed with her.

Let me say something. I'm a firm believer in prayer, but I'm also a firm believer that you do what you have to do when you can do it. The next morning after Heidi left I drove down to the school and talked to the principal. I told the principal what was happening with Gary.

I ended by saying, "When my daughter hurts so bad that she doesn't want to come to this school anymore, how bad does Gary feel?"

The principal looked at me and said, "Thanks for coming in, Mr. Miller. I don't want this happening in my school. I'll take care of it."

Two days later when Heidi came home from school, she walked in and said, "Everything is O.K., Dad."

I said, "What happened?"

"Today the teacher sent Gary down to the office to be the office monitor and when he left she yelled at all of us!"

"Well, what did she say?"

"She told us we'd better stop picking on Gary. She said to quit calling him names. We'd better include him in everything we do, and you know what she said she'd do to us if we didn't?"

I said, "What?"

"She said we were all dead meat!"

"Your teacher said 'dead meat'?"

"Dad, those were the exact words she said. We were dead meat!"

"How did Gary take it?" I asked.

"Dad, Gary came back from the office and some of the kids said, 'Hey, Gary, eat lunch with us.' At recess everybody played four-

square with him. Gosh, Dad, at the end of school Gary was smiling
from ear to ear! You ought to have seen him! He was so happy."
  I said, "That's neat, Heidi."
  I told you that story to say this to you. In the society we live in
we have been taught from our youth up that it is funny to put people
down. It's strange. We have a whole series of put-down words we
inflict upon each other. All you've got to be is a little different. Be a
little shorter, a little taller, a little heavier, a little thinner. Be the first
one to wear glasses. Just be different, and you are fair game, legal
target, to be picked on.
  How many of you — seriously, I want you to raise your hands
for this — how many of you can remember a time since you started
school when you were the butt of the joke and it hurt? It wasn't
funny and you hurt inside. Yeah.
  Let me say this to you. If a person was playing basketball and he
was coming down the court, went up for a shot, came down and
landed wrong on his ankle and broke it, you know what would happen? That person would get carried off the court, and they would
take him in an ambulance to a hospital. The leg would be X-rayed,
they would set the bone, and they'd put it in a cast.
  When people came to school the next week and this guy had a
cast on, everyone would know he had been hurt. Everybody would
know because they could see the cast. They would sign his cast and
somebody would carry his books after class because he'd be on
crutches.
  But you know what happens a lot of times? We start putting
people down, calling them names, and they hurt on the inside where
we can't see the pain. How many times did someone look at Paul
Horne and say, "You're ugly," before he finally believed he was the
ugliest person that ever lived? How much hurt do we inflict on
people because if we don't see a cast, and we don't see blood, and we
don't see a bandage, we don't know the pain that is being inflicted? It
hurts.
  But you know, with the same energy you use to put someone

down, you can make someone feel good.

You can look at someone and say, "You know, you have a great smile."

"I like your outfit."

"I love your hair."

"Is that a new sweater? It looks good on you."

You can pay someone a compliment. But you know what? We give someone a compliment and people get embarrassed. So we don't get very many compliments. But you hear someone being put down and you laugh. That is exactly the opposite of the way it should be.

How many people would it have taken to come up to Paul Horne and say, "You're really a great guy. I really like you," for Paul to be alive today?

Let me say something to you. How many of you truly, honestly, and sincerely would rather have someone give you a compliment than a cut? How many of you would rather have the compliment? Raise your hand high.

Well, if you'd rather have a compliment, give a compliment. Thank you.

SUPPORT SHEET

Date:

FAMILY:

Name   Phone Number

1.

2.

3.

FRIENDS (or friends' parents):

Name   Phone Number

1.

2.

3.

SCHOOL (counselors, teachers, administrators):

Name   Phone Number

1.

2.

COMMUNITY (police officers, firefighters, clergy):

Name   Phone Number

1.

2.

EMERGENCY PROGRAMS (hotlines, teenage talk lines, emergency numbers):

Name   Phone Number

1.

2.

COUNSELORS, PSYCHOLOGISTS, PSYCHIATRISTS:

Name   Phone Number

1.

2.

UPDATE THIS LIST, every six months, if you move, or if you change schools.

FURTHER READING

CHAPTER 1 — INTRODUCTION
Too Young to Die—Youth and Suicide, Francine Klagsbrun, Houghton Mifflin Company, 1984

CHAPTER 2 — WHAT IS DEPRESSION?
The Right to Feel Bad — Coming to Terms with Normal Depression, Lesley Hazleton, Ballantine, 1985
When Bad Things Happen to Good People, Harold S. Kushner, Avon, 1983

CHAPTER 4 — HOW TO TALK TO EACH OTHER
Parents' List:
Liberated Parents/Liberated Children, Elaine Mazlish and Adele Faber, Avon, 1975
How to Talk So Kids Will Listen and Listen So Kids Will Talk, Elaine Mazlish and Adele Faber, Avon, 1982
Between Parent and Teenager, Haim De Ginott, Avon, 1971

Kids' List:
When Living Hurts, Sol Gordon, UAHC, 1985

CHAPTER 6 — DRUG AND ALCOHOL ABUSE
Under the Influence, A Guide to the Myths and Realities of Alcoholism, James Milam and Katherine Ketchan, Madrona Publishing, 1981
Repeat After Me, Claudia Black, M.A.C. Publishing, 1985
My Dad Loves Me, My Dad Has a Disease, Claudia Black, M.A.C. Publishing, 1983

CHAPTER 7 — SEXUAL ABUSE

Help Me Remember . . . Help Me Forget, Robert Sadler and Marie Chapian, Jeremy Books, Bethany Fellowship, 1981

Kiss Daddy Goodnight, Louise Armstrong, Pocket Books, 1978

Mom Take Time, Pat Baker, Baker Book House Company, 1976

The Day the Loving Stopped, Julie Autumn Lift, Seaview Books, 1980

Triumph Over Darkness, Wendy Wood M.A. and Leslie Hatton, Beyond Words, 1989

CHAPTER 8 — LOVE AND RESPECT

The Hug Therapy Book, Kathleen Keating, Minneapolis, CompCare Publishers, 1983

Hug Therapy 2, Kathleen Keating, Minneapolis, CompCare Publishers, 1987

Living, Loving and Learning, Leo Buscaglia, Fawcett, 1983

Pictures of Paul Horne used in the *Dare to Live* program

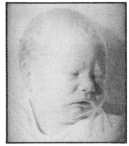

Baby picture of Paul Horne

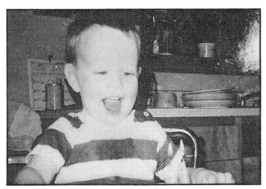

Paul at his second birthday

Paul, age 3, holding football

Paul (in middle) with cousins

Paul and Snowball

Paul riding a donkey at grandfather's farm

Paul on his grandfather's tractor

Paul and his only brother Wayne

Paul, a typical 12-year-old

Paul at age 13

Paul at Christmas

Paul's last picture

Grave site

Funeral wreath

Who Am I?

Paul Horne

My name is Paul. I'm a very shy person. I feel uncomfortable around other people, especially who are better looking than me. I sometimes feel that I'm the ugliest person in the world, that I'm a nobody. I used to be a better person a few years ago. A year ago I began to have problems with my father so I stole his pickup and went to California. I got caught there and in the course of the next two months I was in a lot of trouble. I even tryed to take my life because I felt I had dug myself into a hole so deep that I could never find my way out. All the years that I've been in school I've never had a girlfriend who has really liked me. I'm a nice understanding person. I don't know why they won't give me a chance. I've always wanted to meet a special person who would care about me and love me and I could love and care about her. People say "Just wait, you'll meet that special person some day." I have patience, but I guess I got no faith. I really get depressed at times. I don't believe in God, not anymore anyway. Look, all he has to do is come down hear and show himself and then everyone will worship him. I see no reason for him to put us on this planet. People say he decides whether we go to hell or heaven even before were born, whats he (get) his kicks out of making people, or however, he makes people be born, and then destroying their souls. I see no reason for it. I could write on and on about things but I'll stop now.

Dated 8-6-85